A Guide to West Virginia
Rail Trails

A Guide to West Virginia Rail Trails

Robin Broughton

quarrier press

Charleston, West Virginia

Quarrier Press
Charleston, WV

First Edition

10 9 8 7 6 5 4 3 2 1

Printed in the United States of America

Library of Congress Control Number: 2010932318
ISBN-13: 978-1-891852-71-8
ISBN-10: 1-891852-71-X
Book and cover design: Mark S. Phillips

Editorial Assistants: Mary Katherine Casto, Diane Brown

Distributed by:

West Virginia Book Company
1125 Central Avenue
Charleston, WV 25302
www.wvbookco.com

Dedicated to Kevin Lawrence
May 16, 1960–March 6, 2006

TABLE OF CONTENTS

Thanks to...

Tristan & Keatan Broughton
Paul Broughton
Diane & Richard Brown
Marguaret & Neal Jeffers
Nolan & Benjamin Lawrence
Mary Casto
WV Division of Tourism
DJ Allen
Justin Gaull
Betty Carver
David, Summer & Will Light
Frank Proud
The Greenbrier Suites, Durbin, WV
Steve Jones
North Bend State Park
Jessie Ulderich
North Bend Rail Trail State Park
Rail Trail Conservancy
Katy Miller
Karen Carper
Dave Cline
Ruby Greathouse
Jerry & Joyce Varvarosky
Doug Wayt
Chris Lavenski
Jay Wallace
Ralph Larue
Dan Talbott
Rex Riffle
Tim Miller

Carol Whetsell
Linda Adams
Tim Henry
Shirley Grant
Crysty & William Linkenhoker
Bubby George
Kathleen & John Panek
Gillum House B&B, Shinnston, WV
Mary Willis
Tony & Sydney Michalski
Mike Book
Bill Webb
Dave Watson
Peggy Pings
Barbara Brasher
Jim Hudson
Bill Robinson
Leslee McCarty
Gary & Bonnie Brown
Gail Hyer, Pocahontas County Convention & Visitors Bureau
Bruce & Melisa Donaldson
4 Seasons Resort, Richwood, WV
Jason Starcher
Bob Henry Baber
Mandy & Joey Riddle
Bill Nottingham
Charleston Bicycle Center, Charleston, WV
Brian Willard
Babcock State Park
Dick Morris

Laura Parquette
Snowshoe Mountain Resort,
    Slatyfork, WV
Beth Gill
Ace Adventure Center, Oak Hill,
    WV
Baymont Inn & Suites, Weirton,
    WV
Barb Owens
Highland Scene Tours, Davis,
    WV
Sam Jinks & Diane Baisden
Blackwater Bikes, Davis, WV
The Purple Fiddle, Thomas, WV
Kate & John Bright
Locust Hill BB & Spa,
    Marlinton, WV
Dave & Paula Zorn
Frank O'Brien, Wheeling CVB,
    Wheeling, WV
McClure House Hotel, Wheeling,
    WV
Cindy Johnson
Kelly Pack
Dave Watson
Eagles #344, Wheeling, WV
Diane Jordan
David Wohl
Susan Minnerly
Mike Riley
Amy & Doug Atkins
Amy Tolliver & Scott Duffer
Sarah Crandall-Fletcher & Kevin
    Fletcher
Joel Gibson

Alinda Perrine
The Calwell Practice, Law & Arts
    Center West
Diane Ceraolo
Alyssa Britt
Sharon Kay Phillips
Ella Belling
Clif Bobinski
Duane Nichols
Rachael Stebbins
Olivia Litman

PREFACE

This guidebook is a great resource for discovering West Virginia's rail trails, but it also serves a higher purpose—a guide for introducing your family to nature. Over the past couple of decades, the nation has turned indoors for recreational activity and it's now reflected in our children's physical and mental health. "Nature is increasingly an abstraction you watch on a nature channel," stated Richard Louv in his book *Last Child in the Woods*. In his book, Louv discusses the therapeutic effects of nature and coins the phrase "Nature Deficit Disorder." Thankfully, Robin Broughton left no rail trail untouched in the development of this guidebook. From locating waterfalls and rivers to pointing out the most scenic vistas, this guide identifies the historic and natural phenomenon that must be experienced along each trail.

Fewer and fewer places in America are preserving authentic outdoor experiences. Fortunately, West Virginia is one place where dedicated people are working to preserve and convert old rail beds into trails with the same fortitude as the loggers and miners that initially built them. Each rail trail has its own story to tell, and it's evident in the construction of its bridges, tunnels and friendly villages. Nothing can compare to the eerily exciting experience of riding your bike through an old train tunnel where you feel the cool, damp air embrace you and the only sounds that exist are the echoes of gravel beneath your tires. To discover something is to experience it. Let this book be more than a guide for riding a rail trail. Let it serve as a guide to educate your children and connect them with the sights, sounds, and scents of the nature you grew up with.

Justin Gaull
WV Division of Tourism

INTRODUCTION

For years I snubbed rail trails. I always thought of myself as a "mountain biker"—give me single-track: roots, rocks and speed; tight switchbacks, steep drop-offs and technical climbs.

I managed to avoid rail trails most of my life. I always wondered what could be the fun in riding a wide, basically flat path for miles and miles. To me, it seemed as boring as "going for a Sunday drive."

But then I rode one.

With my daughter Keatan, 4 at the time, on a trailer bike attached to my bike and my 8-year-old son Tristan on his own bike, my family set off to ride the 10-mile Blackwater Canyon Rail Trail from Thomas to Hendricks, West Virginia. My "single-track" mind soon became inundated with things I'd rarely experienced when I was flying through my tight, twisting race course trails.

Not having to focus on my riding gave me time to see what's really there. It was so refreshing just to be able to purely enjoy being on my bike. I didn't have to think about how to shift my weight or when to lift my front wheel off the ground.

We chatted as we rode through fields of vivid wildflowers and past the whitewater rapids of the Blackwater River. We saw coke ovens, where coal was purified during the industrial age to be used as a heating source by the Pittsburgh steel giants. We saw carvings by Italian stonecutters. At one point a deer ran alongside us for about 30 feet.

About five miles into the ride, we heard the roar of a waterfall and decided to explore. Someone had mentioned there was a large waterfall within hiking distance of the trail, and we were hoping we had found it. Sure enough, a short but steep trail brought us to a splendid waterfall. I was in awe as I looked at the 30-foot waterfall. Its powerful white rapids spilled into a pristine, aquamarine pool of water. We navigated through the rocks until we were practically under the waterfall itself. A cool mist of water splashed us as we sat on the rocks and ate our lunch.

It was a beautiful sight. I thought to myself that something as stunning as this is usually roped off with paved steps leading to it. It's the kind of place you usually don't see without entering a state park, obtaining a brochure and following signs. No, this was different. It was so much more incredible than our driving trip to the popular tourist destination, Blackwater Falls, the day before. This waterfall was untouched by humans. There was such satisfaction as the kids and I marveled at what we had found—at what we had come to know only by pedaling along an old railroad route.

Suddenly, what makes for a good bike ride had new meaning to me. Before, I never would have considered a ride "good" if it didn't include a gnarly section or a super-challenging climb. On this ride, I hadn't gotten any real speed. I never encountered a real challenge. Yet I ended up with the same wonderful mixture of excitement, exhilaration and fatigue after this "level" ride than I had from any single-track rides.

This was the inspiration for the book *A Guide to Rail Trails in West Virginia*. And now, almost four years later, I'm proud to say I've ridden rail trails across the state, and found treasures, like this waterfall, in every nook and cranny. In this book, I tell what you can expect from each trail—the distance, the trail roughness, towns you'll pass, rivers you'll travel, places to eat and sleep. But, I have a feeling the best part of your ride will be the unexpected—those hidden gems you're sure to uncover.

BEFORE YOU BIKE/HIKE:

1. Bikers: Check out your rack system. I know from experience how much damage it does to your bike and car when a bike falls off while you're driving. Also be sure to check ahead to see if the hotel or resort where you're staying will allow bicycles in the room. If so, you might want to request a first-floor room so you don't have to carry a bike up and down stairs before and after each ride. Many places, like Snowshoe Resort, offer a "bike check-in," a secure place where you can check your bike in and out.

2. Bikers/Hikers: Be sure to pack enough water. You will need two large water bottles or a full hydration pack for a 2-3 hour ride/hike. Also, put an extra gallon of water in your vehicle. If you forget to fill up your hydration pack or water bottle at the motel and you're driving to a remote location to ride/hike, you will have water. At many state parks, you start at the trailhead, which often has no water source.

3. Bikers/Hikers: Pack high-energy snacks for rides/hikes over two hours. Fig bars, pepperoni rolls, chocolate candies, raisins and crackers with peanut butter all pack well. For extra long rides/hikes, bring energy gels (available at your local bike shop).

4. Bikers/Hikers: Check in at the local bike shop or the park's mountain biking center before heading off on the trails. Most of the time they will provide you with a map and invaluable information about which trails are open, which ones are in good shape, and which ones to avoid. While rail trails are rarely closed, there are times when the water is very high in the tunnels or when bridges are flooded. Often the people in the bike shop are the best ones to choose a ride/hike that matches your ability. When telling them your skill level, be honest. If you don't ride/hike a lot of single-track, you should steer clear of the rail trails that require technical skills (for instance, Williams River and Narrow Gauge) until you gain more experience.

4. Bikers/Hikers: It's a good idea to bring a large sturdy zip-lock bag with you. This will be invaluable for carrying this book and other items you don't want to get wet. While some of the state parks have "waterproof" maps, most simply have paper maps. After a little rain or a few muddy sections, you will no longer be able to read the map if you don't protect it. You should also carry a pen so you can make marks on the map along the way.

5. Bikers/Hikers: Take steps not to get lost. The rail trails are very well marked, so the chances of getting lost are slim. However, if this is to occur on a rail trail or on a side excursion onto single-track trails, follow this advice: When you come to a fork or side trail that is not on the map, logic should prevail. Choose the option that is the best groomed. If there's a choice between an uphill and a downhill (and they are equally groomed), it's more often than not going to be the uphill (unless you are at the end of the ride.) There are lots of quick "outs" to get off the mountain fast; these are side trails and often won't take you back to your vehicle, so beware. When faced with a decision, study the map and try to determine in which direction you should be heading and choose the trail that seems to be going that way. Most importantly, don't panic. By all means, if you do take a wrong turn, try to backtrack. Do not try to find a "new" way out. This is sometimes hard to make yourself do-the memory of all that you have just ridden is fresh in your mind, and it might seem like a long journey back. Don't try to convince yourself that you can find a quicker way. More often than not, you will become more lost.

6. Bikers/Hikers: Use a pedometer/odometer if possible. Though these are rarely calibrated perfectly, they are still very useful. If you are on a 15-mile rail trail, it will be very helpful for you to know when you are at the 5-mile point or the halfway point. This allows you to pace yourself and eliminates a lot of the anxiety you might experience. The other great thing about an odometer is that it gives you total mileage, so you can include this in a riding journal. That way you can look back and see exactly how far you rode and on what date.

7. Bikers/Hikers: Walkie-talkies can really come in handy-especially if you are riding/hiking in a group. This gives people the freedom to ride/hike at their own pace and still be able to communicate with the others. Walkie-talkies with a 5-7 mile range are fairly inexpensive and work quite well.

8. Bikers: Carry the right tools with you. At the very least you need a spare tube, tire levers, a pump (or multiple CO2 charges), and a multi-purpose tool that includes allen wrenches and a chain tool. Better to have a tool and not need it than to need a tool and not have it. Also, you should have a floor pump, a shock pump (if your bike has a suspension), rags, chain lubricant, sunscreen, insect repellent and several old towels in your vehicle.

9. Bikers/Hikers: Especially when riding in the mountains of West Virginia, pack a lightweight shell. Sometimes there are extreme changes in the temperature and storms move especially fast in the mountains. Most shells can be rolled tightly and placed in or tied onto a hydration pack.

Bikers: Maintaining Your Bike

The only thing that can spoil a ride faster than a mechanical problem is a mechanical problem that you could have prevented or fixed. And if you're mountain biking in West Virginia, which often involves riding on primitive trails miles from civilization, a flat tire or a broken chain can be more than just a headache. It can mean a two-hour hike, lugging your 26-pound bike all the way back to your car.

Cleanliness

Clean your bike after each ride. The best way to prevent mechanical problems is to clean and maintain your bike after each ride. Use a hose to rinse off your bike. Avoid using full pressure on the hubs of the wheels. Use a soapy sponge and a small brush to clean off your frame and wheels. Spray a degreaser on the chain and use a chain brush or chain cleaner to scrub down the chain. Most chain brushes have a curved-tooth end that you can use to dig out grime from in between the cogs. Use a rag to dry it thoroughly. Oil the chain with a lubricant.

Pre-ride Checks

Prevention is the best cure. Before each ride, check the air pressure in both tires, using a tire gauge. If the pressure in either tire is under the recommended amount, add more air. To determine the recommended pressure, check the tire's sidewall for the recommended psi. The range is usually between 35-65 psi. Also check the front and rear braking effectiveness. If your brakes do not hit the rims before the brake lever is halfway through its travel, adjust them by twisting the brake adjuster (found on the brake lever) out (counter-clockwise). Make sure the two quick releases on your wheels and the quick release on your seat are clamped tightly.

Flats

Bikers dread one sound more than any other. It's sort of a "pop" followed by an evil "hiss." Yes, the air is slowly leaking out of your tire. To replace a flat tube with a good tube, first open the quick release and disconnect the brake straddle cable. Remove the wheel by pushing the quick release lever out. Unscrew the valve cap. If the valve looks like the one on your car, then it is a Schrader valve. Otherwise, it's a presta valve. If it's a Schrader, use a small allen wrench to depress the pin in the center to allow the remaining air out. If it's a presta, loosen the valve nut and push the exposed pin to force any remaining air out. Use tire levers to pry one side of the tire loose from the rim. Then, pull the damaged tire out. Run your finger along the inside of the tire, removing any thorns or sharp objects. If the sidewall of the tire is torn you can wrap a dollar bill around the new tube where it will contact the sidewall tear. Add some air to the tire – just enough to give the tube some form. Place the valve of the new tube through the rim and run the tube around the inside of the tire. Use your fingers to place the edge of the tire back into the rim. If it becomes too tight, use the tire levers to aid you, being careful not to pinch the new tube. Next, pump up the new tube. Tighten the valve. Replace the valve nut and screw on the valve cap. To patch a tube, follow the same steps but instead of adding the new tube, find the hole in the old tube by pumping it up and listening for leaking air. Then cover the hole with a patch. If your patch is not self-adhesive, you will have to apply some glue.

DISCLAIMER

Neither the publisher nor the author assumes any liability for accidents happening to, or injuries sustained by, readers who engage in the activities described in this book. Readers should keep in mind that odometer readings may vary due to factors beyond the author's control. Such factors might include varying distances and routes chosen to and from the parking area, differences and inaccuracies in calibration of the odometer used by the author/readers, and at times slight differences in distance along the trail due to stops and backtracking for photography. Readers should be advised to use the odometer readings as a guide for approximate distances. Maps in the book may not be exact and should not be your sole source during your trips. Ideally, bring several different map sources with you on your trip.

Also, denotations for the availability of food and water and denotations for access points were accurate at the time the book was written. Over time, these will change. Bikers/hikers should not count on the availability of food and water and should keep in mind that access points may change over time due to weather or other factors. Please note that either the author or photographer rode all 30 of the rail trails covered in this book. Many of these trails were ridden by both of us at the same time, some separately. All descriptions are written as "we" for the purposes of consistency.

Tips for Bikers:

1. Make sure your bike is trail-ready. I highly recommend buying a bike from a bike shop rather than a discount superstore. Bike-shop quality bikes are lighter (this means less energy exerted by you to get where you are going). Plus, most bike shops offer free or very inexpensive tune-ups for the first year you own the bike. This can come in really handy. If, in addition to rail trails, you are going to be doing a good deal of single-track riding, consider purchasing a bike with a front suspension fork. This will make for more comfortable riding and will make it easier to ride over obstacles. People often ask me what brands of bikes I recommend. All of the major brands (Trek, Specialized, Cannondale, etc.) are fairly equal. Test ride a few different brands; it may come down to whichever one "feels" better. Make sure the bike you purchase has knobby tires, good brakes, quick-release wheels (easier for transporting your bike and for changing a flat tire) and a comfortable seat. For off-road riding, the big gel seats are not necessarily the most practical. There will be times you will need to get behind your seat; a narrow seat makes this a lot easier.

2. Buy a bike that fits you properly. I can't tell you how many people I see on bikes that are too big or too small for them. On a mountain bike, you should be able to stand over the top tube with two-three inches of clearance. If your bike is too big, you will be less comfortable riding over technical sections. Also, make sure you can bend your elbows while holding the handlebars. You want to be able to maintain a relaxed posture when riding on trails; if your arms are locked, it will make riding less comfortable and can lead to injury. Adjust your seat so that your leg when it is in its most extended position on the pedal has a slight bend at the knee. If your seat is too low or too high, you may feel some pain in your knees. Riding with your seat as high as possible (while still having a slight bend at your knee) will allow you to pedal most efficiently.

3. Invest in a good helmet. Don't even consider riding without a helmet. I have seen many a cracked helmet (that would have been a cracked skull had the rider not been wearing the helmet). Your helmet is something you will wear on every ride, so make sure you get one that fits properly. Most often, I see people with helmets that are too small for them, that sit "on top" of their heads. Helmets should also protect your forehead. A good test is to see if your forehead is exposed when wearing the helmet; if so, the helmet is too small. If the helmet slides from side to side, it is too big. For a few extra bucks, it makes sense to get a helmet that's lightweight and has plenty of air ventilation. Get full instruction on how to adjust your helmet before taking it home; sometimes the adjustment is not as easy as it looks.

4. You will also need water bottles or a hydration pack. I recommend the hydration pack for off-road riding simply because it allows you to drink without removing your hands from the handlebars for an extended period of time. On trails it's much easier to quickly stick the "tube" in your mouth than to reach down and grab a water bottle, pull it open with your teeth, tip it up for a drink and then replace it. Also hydration packs are great for packing tools and snacks. Most mountain bikers also use gloves (helps sweaty hands grip handlebars, protects against blisters, and protects hands during wrecks) and off-road riding shoes (with a stiffer sole for more power and control).

5. On rougher sections of rail trail (such as Williams River and Narrow Gauge), **try to stay relaxed.** Remember that speed is your friend—meaning that if you're able to keep up your momentum, it will be easier to roll over the rocks and roots. It helps to visualize yourself riding over the obstacles and to tell yourself your front wheel can easily roll over almost anything on the trail. Once you hesitate or slow your speed, you will break your rhythm and most likely "dab" (put your foot down). You should practice trying to "clear" as much of the trail as you can—trying to decrease your number of "dabs" each time.

6. On gradual down hill sections, put your butt back toward the rear of your seat so your arms are stretched out. Brake evenly. Too much front brake (left brake lever) can make you fly over your handlebars (a header); too much rear brake (right brake lever) can make your rear tire skid behind you, causing you to lose control. Practice lightly squeezing both brakes in and out at the same time and maintaining control. Be sure to look 10-20 feet in front of you—you should be looking at what's coming, not focusing on what is right beneath your tires. Look at where you want to go. If you look at where you don't want to go—trust me, you will go there! Our bikes follow our line of vision.

7. On gradual up hills, find a gear that allows you to spin comfortably. Most likely this will be your middle ring in the front. Your legs should not be spinning too fast (this wastes energy and will fatigue you); on the other hand, you should not be working your leg muscles hard to make the pedals turn (this wears out your muscles and will make your legs too sore to ride very far). Basically, the workout part of mountain biking is a combination of strength and cardiovascular. You want to find the perfect cadence that balances the strength required and the cardiovascular (heart-lung) required. If it is a long climb, stand a few times while pedaling to stretch out. Make sure you move your fingers and toes around and stretch your neck as well. Long climbs are a good time to eat an energy bar or gel.

8. Remember that mountain biking is 20% strength, 20% cardiovascular, 10% skill and 50% mental. (Of course, I made those statistics up, but I stand by them!) So much of how well you ride will depend on what you are telling yourself in your mind. Visualize yourself as a strong rider. Learn to love your bike and have confidence in its abilities.

INTERNATIONAL MOUNTAIN BIKING ASSOCIATION RULES

The IMBA is an organization that is concerned with land access issues. In many areas of the country, federal lands and parks have been closed to mountain bikes. The IMBA is attempting to prevent further closures and keep riding areas accessible to mountain bikers. Here are the guidelines:

Ride on open trails only. Respect trail and road closures (ask if not sure): avoid possible trespass on private land; obtain permits and authorization as may be required. Federal and state wilderness areas are closed to cycling. Leave no trace. Be sensitive to dirt beneath you. Even on open trails, you should not ride where you will leave evidence of your passing, such as certain soils shortly after a rain.

Observe the different types of soils and trail construction; practice low-impact cycling. This also means staying on the trail and not creating any new ones. Be sure to pack out at least as much trash as you pack in. Control your bicycle! Inattention for even a second can cause disaster. Excessive speed maims and threatens people; there is no excuse for it! Always yield the trail. Make known your approach well in advance. A friendly greeting is considerate and works well; startling someone may cause loss of trail access. Show your respect when passing others by slowing to a walk or even stopping. Anticipate that other trail users may be around corners or in blind spots.

Never spook animals. All animals are startled by an unannounced approach, a sudden movement, or a loud noise. This can be dangerous for you, for others, and for the animals. Give animals extra room and time to adjust to you. In passing, use special care and follow the directions of horseback riders (ask if uncertain). Running cattle and disturbing wild animals is a serious offense. Leave gates as you found them, or as marked.

Plan ahead. Know your equipment, and the area in which you are riding—and prepare accordingly. Be self-sufficient at all times. Wear a helmet, keep your bike in good condition, and carry necessary supplies for changes in weather or other conditions. A well-executed trip is a satisfaction to you and not a burden or offense to others.

WEATHER AND SAFETY PRECAUTIONS

West Virginia weather has multiple personalities, not all of which are friendly. Mountain ranges snag storm systems as they attempt to cross the state, suddenly wringing torrents of water from the clouds. Even on the nicest of days, a storm can come from nowhere and spoil your day if you are not prepared. Since the weather patterns generally move west to east, the western slopes and valleys have high annual precipitation, while the eastern slopes are usually much drier. Some areas in the higher elevations have seen freezing temperatures in all twelve months.

According to the National Weather Service in Charleston, May and October are usually the best months for outdoor activities in West Virginia. These months usually have the calmest, driest weather – between the winter and summer storms. Batty suggests that in order to get the most localized and current weather information, use the National Weather Service's Weather Radio, which can be tuned in around the 162.4 mark on the dial of a VHF frequency radio. Statewide weather information can also be obtained by calling 304-342-7771 between 8 a.m. and 4 p.m. during the week.

Following are some of the National Weather Service tips for weather-related hazards.

Flash Floods: During heavy rains, avoid areas subject to flooding, such as dips, low spots, canyons, and washes. Do not attempt to cross streams. Do not camp along streams and washes during threatening conditions.

Lightning: Most deaths due to lightning occur in the summer months, during the afternoon and early evening. To estimate the distance in miles between you and the lightning flash, count the seconds between the lightning and the thunder and divide by five. If you can hear thunder, you are close enough to the storm to be struck by lightning. If no sturdy shelter or car is nearby, find a low spot—away from trees, fences, and poles—that is not subject to flooding. If you are in the woods, take shelter under the shortest trees. If you feel your skin tingle or your hair stand on end, squat low to the ground on the balls of your feet. Place your hands on your knees with your head between them. Make yourself the smallest target possible, and minimize your contact with the ground.

Winter Storm: If caught in a winter storm while biking, try to find shelter, stay dry, and cover all exposed parts of the body. If shelter is not readily available, build a lean-to, wind break, or snow cave for protection from the wind. Build a fire: it will supply heat and attract attention. Place rock around the fire to absorb and reflect the heat. Melt snow before drinking it, or it will lower your body temperature.

Heat and sun: Cyclists should carry two water bottles and drink plenty of liquids at regular intervals to avoid dehydration. Heat exhaustion and heat stroke are always possible during the warmer months. Heat exhaustion is characterized by cool, moist, pale or flushed skin; heavy sweating, headache; nausea or vomiting; dizziness; and exhaustion. Heat stroke is characterized by hot, red skin; changes in consciousness; rapid, weak pulse; and shallow breathing. Body temperatures can be very high. In either situation, get the victim to a cooler place. With heat exhaustion, remove or loosen tight clothing, and apply cool, wet cloths if available. Give the person cool water to drink, and see that they drink slowly—about half a glass every 15 minutes. Heat stroke is serious, even life-threatening, so get help right away. Quickly cool the body by immersing the victim in cool water. Keep the person lying down and as cool as possible. If the victim is vomiting or losing consciousness, do not give him anything to drink.

Weather becomes a critical issue when out on a bike in the middle of nowhere. Because of a number of possibilities, (among them unpredictable weather, injuries, and bike trouble) it's best not to bike alone. However, if you prefer solitary rides, ride trails you are familiar with, let someone know where you plan to bike, and check in with them when you return.

HUNTING SEASON

Biking amid a horde of hunters is obviously hazardous. Many state parks and forests are open to hunters, as is most of the Monongahela National Forest. If you are biking during the primary hunting seasons— deer and turkey—wear neon or brightly colored clothing; respect others in the woods; use common sense and an eagle eye. Currently hunting is not allowed on Sundays in West Virginia, making this a great day to ride. Following are the hunting seasons in West Virginia:

Small game season: First Saturday in October through December 31.
Deer season (rifle): Monday before Thanksgiving for two weeks.
Spring gobbler season: The third week in April through the third week in May.

In addition to trail information, this book also contains suggestions on where to stay and local points of interest. It is designed to offer a few options and is by no means comprehensive. For the most accurate and up-to-date information, check with the state through the toll-free tourism number, 1-800-CALL-WVA.

TRAIL USES:

B-Biking (recreational mountain bike appropriate)
Mt.B-Mountain Biking (Sturdy mountain bike with knobby tires required).
H-Hiking
E-Equestrian
A-Handicapped Accessible
X-Cross-Country Ski

S-Skate
F-Likely availability of food
W-Likely availability of water

TRAIL RATINGS

Scenery Ratings

★ Not a scenic ride/hike or one with a few scenic points worth noting

★★ A fairly scenic ride/hike

★★★ A very scenic ride/hike characterized by overlooks, vistas and/or bodies of water throughout much of the ride/hike.

★★★★ A magnificently scenic ride/hike characterized by overlooks, vistas, and/or bodies of water throughout most or all of the ride/hike.

Trail Roughness:

★ Paved or smooth asphalt trail; appropriate for road bike or mountain bike and most hikers.

★★ Mostly smooth with some rough spots containing gravel or other loose rock; mountain bike required; appropriate for most hikers.

★★★ Varied roughness with a majority of the trail containing gravel or other loose rock; mountain bike required; appropriate for hikers with some experience.

★★★★ Very rough trail; often narrow in sections with large rocks and roots and/or water crossings and hike-a-bike sections; sturdy mountain bike with knobby tires required; technical riding skills required; appropriate for advanced hikers.

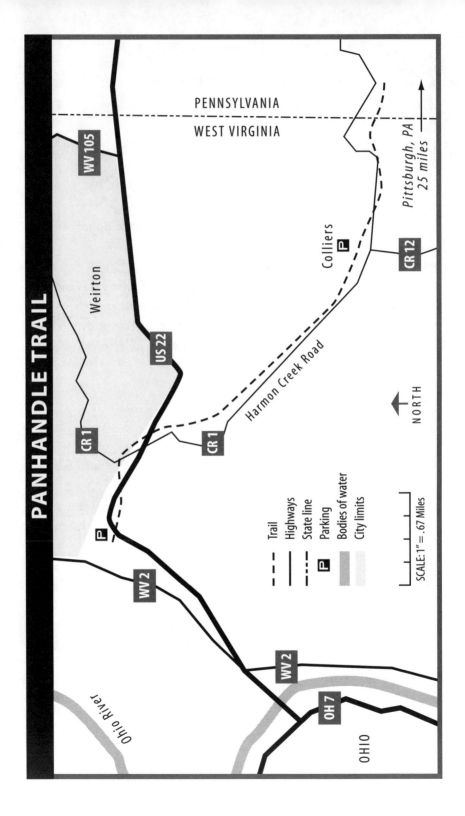

PANHANDLE TRAIL

PENNSYLVANIA

WEST VIRGINIA

WV 105

Weirton

US 22

CR 1

CR 1

Harmon Creek Road

Colliers

P

CR 12

Pittsburgh, PA
25 miles

NORTH

P

WV 2

WV 2

OH 7

OHIO

Ohio River

Trail
Highways
State line
P   Parking
Bodies of water
City limits

SCALE: 1" = .67 Miles

1. PANHANDLE RAIL TRAIL

This Northern Panhandle trail is West Virginia's link to the rest of the country's rail trail system. Hop on the Panhandle Rail Trail and ride to Pittsburgh (about 29 miles) or all of the way to Washington, DC if you like. While West Virginia only owns four miles of this trail, the state's volunteers actively maintain not only their own state's section—but also all of the way to Pittsburgh. Volunteers hold weekly trail maintenance get-togethers, which are usually well attended.

The Panhandle Trail is named after the Panhandle Division of the Pennsylvania Railroad, the abandoned rail line upon which it is built. The trail opened in 2000, and is the first interstate trail in West Virginia.

The trail begins in Weirton, at Harmon Creek Road, where you will ride/hike under a large Panhandle Trails sign mounted to a bridge. The trail follows Harmon Creek as it twists its way toward the state border. You'll pass through charming country neighborhoods with people who support the trail. We spotted one man who had placed a chair next to his newspaper box, where he spent mornings reading his *Weirton Daily Times* and watching cyclists pass by.

You'll pass through the village of Colliers about ¾ a mile before you reach the Pennsylvania border. There is a place for parking and a picnic table here.

We got a kick out of the stone marker telling us we had crossed from West Virginia into Pennsylvania; the marker is the original marker used by the former railroad, with West Virginia written vertically on one side and Pennsylvania on the other.

The easiest access to the trail is in Weirton. We stayed at the Baymont Inn & Suites in Weirton, which was super convenient, located just one exit east of the trailhead. The motel was also close to Deejay's BBQ Ribs & Grille, which was the best "after-ride" food you could hope for.

Length: 4 miles to state line, 29 miles to Pittsburgh, PA
Surface: Packed limestone

Allowed Uses: H, B, X, E
County: Brooke
Endpoints: Weirton and Pennsylvania state line, or on to Pittsburgh area
Access Points: Weirton F/W (food & water), convenience stores (not accessible directly from trail)
Contact: Weirton Parks & Recreation 304-797-8520, www.panhandletrail.org
Trail Roughness: ★★
Scenery: ★★

Directions:
   From Charleston, WV: Take I-77 North to Exit 44A, merging onto I-70 East. Take I-70 East to Ohio Rt. 7 North, the last exit before crossing the Ohio River. Follow Ohio Rt. 7 about 26 miles to US 22 East. Cross the Ohio River on US 22 East into West Virginia. Exit US 22 East at the third West Virginia exit, and turn left at Harmon Creek Road. The trailhead parking is about 300 yards on the right side of Harmon Creek Road.
   From Pittsburgh, PA: Follow US 22 West about 35 miles toward West Virginia. Exit US 22 at the third West Virginia exit, Harmon Creek

Road; then turn right onto Harmon Creek Road. The trailhead parking is about 300 yards ahead, on the right side of Harmon Creek Road.

From Columbus, OH: Follow I-70 East 130 miles to Ohio Rt. 7 North, the last exit before crossing the Ohio River. Follow Ohio Rt. 7 North about 26 miles to US 22 East. Cross the Ohio River on US 22 East into West Virginia. Exit US 22 East at the third West Virginia exit, at Harmon Creek Road, and then turn left onto Harmon Creek Road. The trailhead parking is about 300 yards on the right side of Harmon Creek Road.

From Wheeling, WV: Follow Rt. 2 North 25 miles to US 22 East. Follow US 22 East about two miles, and exit at the second exit, Harmon Creek Road. From the exit, turn left onto Harmon Creek Road. The trailhead parking is about 300 yards on the right side of Harmon Creek Road.

WHERE TO STAY AND DINE:

Baymont Inn & Suites
1 Amerihost Drive
Weirton, WV 26062
800-434-5800

Deejay's Barbecue Ribs & Grille
380 Three Springs Drive
Weirton, WV 26062
304-748-1150

Memories Sports Grille
1229 Pennsylvania Avenue
Weirton, WV 26062
304-797-8777

Mountaineer Cafe
100 Taylor Avenue
Weirton, WV 26062
304-740-3410

Holiday Inn
350 Three Springs Road
Weirton, WV 26032
304-723-5522

Fairfield (Marriott)
Three Springs Road
Weirton, WV 26032
304-723-0088

Town House Motel (2 miles
west of Harmon Creek Exit /
Panhandle trailhead)
4147 Freedom Way
Weirton, WV 26062
304-748-2260

2. WELLSBURG YANKEE RAIL TRAIL

Though short in length at just 2 miles, this paved trail gives you a nice 16-block tour of the charming town of Wellsburg, a town that's claim-to-fame is having been the home of Patrick Gass, the last surviving member of the Lewis & Clark expedition and author of its journal. He died at age 99, just two months shy of his 100th birthday.

The trail connects to the Brooke Pioneer Trail (6.9 miles), so make the ride as long as 8.9 miles one way if you like.

If you are planning on just riding the more substantial Brooke Pioneer Trail System, we recommend making the small effort to include the Wellsburg-Yankee tour of the quiet Ohio River town and its countryside. Like the railroads of yesteryear, the trail winds along the outskirts of people's backyards and past old warehouses, where the trains used to load and unload.

We rode this in the fall when the vivid orange and red leaves were stunning. The trail links to the Brooke Pioneer Trail at the bridge that goes across Buffalo Creek. This bridge was originally constructed for

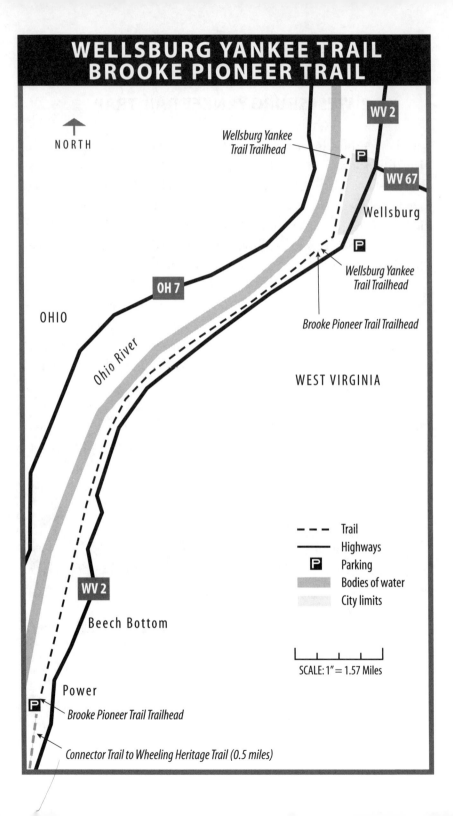

WELLSBURG YANKEE TRAIL
BROOKE PIONEER TRAIL

NORTH

Wellsburg Yankee
Trail Trailhead

WV 2

WV 67

Wellsburg

Wellsburg Yankee
Trail Trailhead

Brooke Pioneer Trail Trailhead

OH 7

OHIO

Ohio River

WEST VIRGINIA

Trail
Highways
Parking
Bodies of water
City limits

WV 2

Beech Bottom

SCALE: 1" = 1.57 Miles

Power

Brooke Pioneer Trail Trailhead

Connector Trail to Wheeling Heritage Trail (0.5 miles)

the Panhandle Railroad Company's first Steubenville to Wheeling run, February 24, 1878.

Length: 2 miles
Surface: Asphalt
Allowed Uses: H, B, S, A
County: Brooke
Endpoints: WV 67, and 30th Street
Access Points: Yankee Street, Wellsburg F/W available at various points as you ride the two miles through Wellsburg on the trail
Trail roughness: ★
Scenery: ★ ★

Directions:

From Charleston, WV: Take I-77 toward Parkersburg (Crosses into OH). Merge onto I-70 E via Exit 44A toward Wheeling (Crosses into WV). Take the Main St/US 40E/WV 2 N exit, Exit 1A, toward downtown. Turn slight right onto US 40/WV 2 S/Main Street. Turn left onto US 40/10th Street. Turn left onto US 40/WV 2 N/Market Street. Turn left onto US 40 W/WV 2 N/7th Street. Turn right onto WV 2/Main Street. Continue to follow WV 2 North. End at Wellsburg. Enter Wellsburg on WV 2. The trail runs north-south through town with the river to your west. Access to this trail from any street in Wellsburg. Note that this trail connects to Brooke Pioneer Rail trail at the south end.

WHERE TO STAY AND DINE:

Lu's Motel
215 Commerce Street Ext
Wellsburg, WV 26070
304-737-4251

Town House Motel
4147 Freedom Way
Weirton, WV 26062
304-748-2260

Station Grill
1200 Commerce Street
Wellsburg, WV 26070
304-737-0730

Kroger (adjacent to Yankee Trail)
91 - 27th Street
Wellsburg, WV 26070
304-243-6230

3. BROOKE PIONEER TRAIL SYSTEM

This 6.9-mile trail (with a 3-mile gap to be paved in the future) is marked every 1/10 of a mile—with a bench often in sight. The trail is heavily used by senior citizens and by patients who are recovering from heart procedures or other surgeries. The trail not only has more mileage signage than any other rail trail in the state, but also has a fair amount of signs noting historic sites and plant life. A sign pointing to the largest American Elm Tree east of the Mississippi River was an especially interesting find.

Mile marker 0 is parallel with State Route 2 (which runs alongside the Ohio River) at the Brooke/Ohio County line at Short Creek. The markers count south to north, same as and parallel with State Route 2. These have been very useful for emergency vehicles responding to calls on the trail, knowing it is the same as the highway. The current northern end is at the 6.9-mile marker at the south edge of Wellsburg and the Yankee Trail. North of Wellsburg, the Pioneer Trail parallels

and matches mile markers with the state road system, continuing north as constructed to the Panhandle Trail.

The trail has lots of views of river industry but just as many beautiful spots along the way. After about 3 miles, you will come to a "No Trespassing" sign, where you'll have to ride/hike the road for the next 3 miles. Even with some road riding experience, this made us a bit nervous, as the traffic on WV 2 was heavy and the shoulder was tight.

This 3.4-mile detour is

temporary. Land has been acquired by private investors, who already have applied for funds to complete this trail section. At the time of book publication, volunteers were working on finishing this section. Hopefully, by the time you read this, the detour will be eliminated. We got back on the trail where the 2-lane road becomes a 4-lane road and continued south toward Pike Island Dam, which has parking and restrooms.

The cut sandstone walls between markers 4 and 6 were put in place for the Panhandle Traction Co. (street cars) around 1901. It was in place to keep streetcar tracks from collapsing onto the Panhandle Railroad tracks beside it. The wall is under the watchful eye of the State Department of Culture and History.

The Brooke Pioneer Trail's "to scale" 'Planet Walk' is presently marked on the pavement. The Sun is at Buffalo Creek, immediately south of Wellsburg. Planets are from there to the south. Pluto is 3.7 miles south of the Sun, at the 3.0 Mile Marker in Beech Bottom.

Parking is available along Route 2, immediately south of Wellsburg, on the north beside Smith Gas Station. Parking is also available near Route 2, immediately north of the Brooke/Ohio County line at Short Creek, 0.2 Mile Marker, across from Airport Road.

The southern end of the trail at Pike Island Dam has a half-mile connector to the Wheeling Heritage Rail trail.

Length: 6.9 miles
Surface: Asphalt
Allowed Uses: H, B, S, A
County: Brooke, Ohio
Endpoints: Wellsburg and Pike Island Dam
Access Points: Trailheads on WV 2/ food and water at the north end
Contact: Ruby Greathouse 304-737-0506,
   www.brookepioneertrail.org
Trail Roughness: ★
Scenery: ★★

Directions:

From Charleston, WV: Take I-77 toward Parkersburg (Crosses into OH). Merge onto I-70 E via Exit 44A toward Wheeling (Crosses into WV). Take the Main St/US 40E/WV 2 N exit, Exit 1A, toward downtown. Make a slight right onto US 40/WV 2 S/Main Street. Turn left onto US 40/10th Street. Turn left onto US 40/WV 2 N/Market Street. Turn left onto US 40 W/WV 2 N/7th Street. Turn right onto WV 2/Main Street. Continue to follow WV 2 N. The southern trailhead begins about 1/10 mile south of Wellsburg on WV 2. From the south, the trailhead is on the right; from the north it is on the left. The trail is clearly marked and parking is available at the entrance.

To Pike Island Dam/Beech Bottom trailhead: The northern trailhead begins at the north end of Beech Bottom on WV 2. From the south the trailhead will be on the left. You will see a sign for the trail.

WHERE TO STAY AND DINE:

Blue Chip Motel
215 Commerce Street Ext
Wellsburg, WV 26070
304-737-4251

Station Grille
1200 Commerce Street
Wellsburg, WV 26070
304-737-0730

Scores Restaurant
1200 Commerce Street
Wellsburg, WV 26070
304-737-1811

4. WHEELING HERITAGE RAIL TRAIL

The Wheeling Heritage Trail exemplifies the best in rail trails—with more than 15 miles of paved trails, passing through an urban setting with various historic landmarks and a myriad of scenic areas. Add a wonderful downtown setting with everything from a vaudeville theatre to the Capitol Music Hall and you have a great vacation getaway. The two-part Wheeling Heritage trail includes the Ohio River Trail, which runs north-south starting at the city line in South Wheeling and traveling 13 miles north to just past the Pike Island Dam.

The Wheeling Creek Trail runs east-west for about five miles, beginning in downtown Wheeling. The first day we started the trail in downtown Wheeling near the Wesbanco Arena and followed the river north to Pike Island Dam and backtracked back to town (about 8 miles each way). Heading north from Wheeling you will soon see a National Historic Landmark, the Wheeling Suspension Bridge, which was the first bridge to cross the Ohio River and the longest bridge in the world when it was completed in 1849. You will also get a great look at the river traffic at the locks at Pike Island. This trail is obviously well loved and used frequently by local folks; while on our ride we saw a power plant worker on rollerblades and quite a few people walking.

The second day, we started at the same spot and rode the trail south to the end of the trail near 48th Street, backtracked to town, and then rode the Wheeling Creek Trail west to east, again backtracking to town (a few miles round trip). While it sounds like a lot of out-and-back, the routes actually seemed perfect both days, and there was never a dull moment.

On the shorter southern section of the trail, you will find nice river views and rustic buildings, including one with "Mail Pouch" painted on the side. Both the northern and southern sections include lots of good historic markers, pointing out highlights along the way.

The Wheeling Creek Trail (about 5 miles each way) connects to the Ohio River Trail at Heritage Point in Wheeling, obviously following

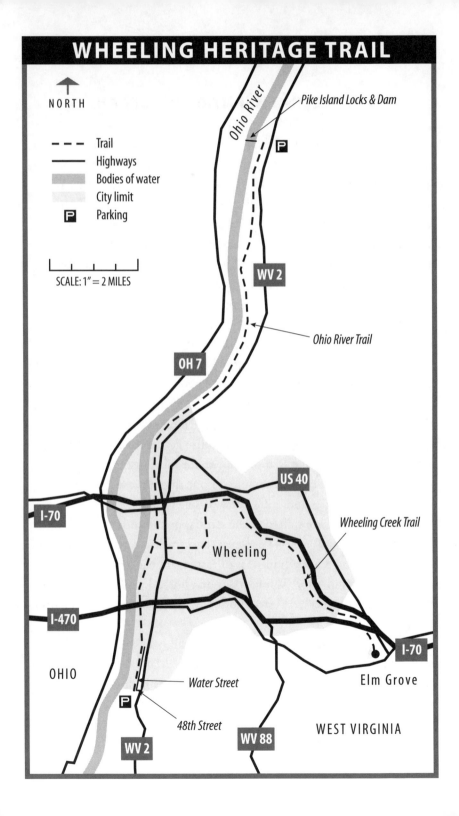

Wheeling Creek. You will ride/hike along the quite lovely creek. The trail parallels I-70. It is a bit noisy, but still has the feel of being in nature.

You will go through the Hempfield Tunnel after riding/hiking across the Hempfield Viaduct (on the National Historic Registry of Bridges), built in 1853 with five 45-foot spans, high above the creek. We passed a couple carrying fishing rods/gear, walking along the trail to their favorite fishing spot. We also spotted some exercise stations along the way (with chin-up bars and other equipment). This part of the trail finishes in Elm Grove, where there is a pretty awesome skateboard park.

Though seven railroads served the city in the 19th century—including the Baltimore & Ohio, the Wheeling & Lake Erie, the Pittsburgh Wheeling & Kentucky, the Hempfield, the Panhandle, the Ohio River & Western and the Pennsylvania Railroad—there is no active railroad in Wheeling today.

We stayed in the McClure Hotel in the heart of downtown Wheeling. Within walking distance were several clubs and live music offerings, as well as the Centre Market, which offers amazing food at great prices.

Length: 17 miles for Ohio River Trail, 5 miles for Wheeling Creek Trail
Surface: Asphalt
Allowed Uses: H, B, S, A
County: Ohio
Endpoints: Pike Island Dam and downtown Wheeling to Elm Grove
Access Points for Ohio River Trail: Pike Island Dam, Rt. 2 north of Warwood, First Street in North Wheeling F/W, 5th Street in North Wheeling F/W, 12th Street at Heritage Point F/W, 14th Street at Heritage Point F/W, 24th Street in Center Wheeling F/W, 35th Street in South Wheeling F/W, 48th Street in South Wheeling F/W.
Access Points for Wheeling Creek Trail: 14th Street at Heritage Port F/W, 17th Street in East Wheeling F/W, Rock Point Road F/W, Washington Avenue in Clator, Lava Avenue in Elm Grove
Note: Follows Ohio River N-S and Wheeling Creek E-W. Downtown section is routed onto bike lanes on the streets.
Contact: Wheeling Convention & Visitors Bureau, 304-233-7709,

www.wheelingcvb.com or 800-828-3097

Trail Roughness: ★
Scenery: ★★

Directions:

From Charleston, WV: Take I-77 North to Exit 44A, merging onto I-70 East to Wheeling. Take Exit 1A and follow the exit ramp onto Main Street. Go two blocks to 12th Street and turn right. This leads you directly to Heritage Port, the town's river front park. Parking is available along nearby Waters Street or in the Wheeling CVB Center Garage on 14th Street and Main Street. Maps are available at the Wheeling CVB. From Heritage Point you can go north or south; this follows WV 2.

From Pittsburgh, PA: Take I-79 South to Washington, PA. Take Exit 38 onto I-70 West. Take a slight left onto I-470 West (towards Columbus). Take Exit 1 toward WV 2. Turn right toward 26th Street. Take 26th Street to Main Street and turn right. Follow Main Street till 12th Street, where you turn right. This leads you directly to Heritage Port, the town's river front park. Parking is available along nearby Waters Street or in the Wheeling CVB Center Garage on 14th Street and Main Street. Maps are available at the Wheeling CVB. From Heritage Point you can go north or south; this follows WV 2.

From Columbus, OH: Follow I-70 East about 130 miles. Take Exit 1A and follow the exit ramp right onto Main Street. Go two blocks to 12th Street and turn right. This leads you directly to Heritage Port, the town's river front park. Parking is available along nearby Waters Street or in the Wheeling CVB Center Garage on 14th Street and Main Street. Maps are available at the Wheeling CVB. From Heritage Point you can go north or south; this follows WV 2.

WHERE TO STAY AND DINE:

McClure House Hotel
1200 Market Street
Wheeling, WV 26003
304-232-0300

River City Restaurant
1400 Main Street
Wheeling, WV 26003
304-233-4555

DiCarlo's Pizza
3111 Main Street
Wheeling, WV 26003
304-233-0730

Tiki Bar and Grill
1201 Market Street
Wheeling, WV 26003
204-233-3499

Hall of Fame Cafe
29 20th Street
Wheeling, WV 26003
304-232-7990

Centre Market
2200 Market Street
Wheeling, WV 26003
304-234-3878

Coleman Fish Market ("The Country's Best Fish Sandwich" - *Gourmet
Magazine* June, 2001)
2226 Market Street
at Centre Market
Wheeling, WV 26003
304-232-8510

Later Alligator (crêperie and great sandwiches and salads; in warm weather
additional outside eating in private back)
2145 Market Street
Wheeling, WV 26003
304-233-1606

Saseen's Restaurant
2149 Market Street
Wheeling, WV 26003
304-232-3690

OTHER:

Wheeling Artisan Center (handcrafted local and regional fine art and crafts)
1400 Main Street
2nd Floor
Wheeling, WV 26003
304-232-1810

Eckhart House Victorian Home Tour & Shop
810 Main Street
Wheeling, WV 26003
304-232-5439

West Virginia Independence Hall
Civil War Historic Site & Museum
1528 Market Street
Wheeling, WV 26003
304-238-1300

Artworks Around Town
2200 Market Street
Wheeling, WV 26003
304- 233-7540

Capitol Theatre (Capitol Music Hall)
1015 Main Street
Wheeling, WV 26003
304-233-7709

The Museums of Oglebay Institute
The Burton Center
Wheeling, WV 26003
304-242-7272

5. GLEN DALE TO MOUNDSVILLE TRAIL

(also called Marshall County Intermodal Rail Trail)

This paved trail, complete with divider lines, is super nice, easy rail trail riding or hiking, perfect for families and other recreational users. Your ride/hike will take you down a path paralleling WV 2 to the east and the Ohio River to the west with several creek crossings. This is a park-to-park ride/hike—starting at Glen Dale City Park on the north end, and going south to Moundsville Riverview Park.

The trail does include about a mile of riding/hiking through city streets, but it is well marked and easy to maneuver. We could not help but be awe-stricken as we rode into Riverview Park and saw the giant green arch of the majestic Moundsville Bridge, which connects the town to rural Belmont County, Ohio.

Moundsville gets its name from the many Adena burial mounds constructed more than 1,000 years ago in that area. Today Moundsville is commonly associated with the famous and now closed West Virginia Penitentiary, which many claim is haunted. If you can make the time, a tour of the Penitentiary would be worth your while.

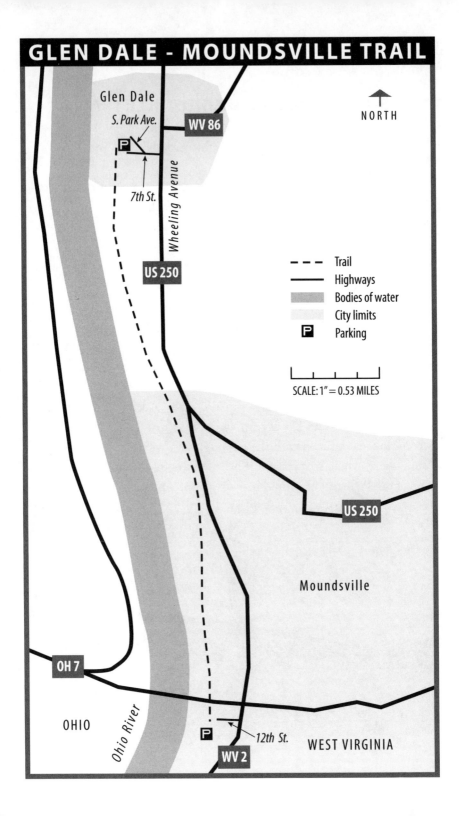

GLEN DALE - MOUNDSVILLE TRAIL

Glen Dale

S. Park Ave.

WV 86

7th St.

Wheeling Avenue

US 250

NORTH

- - - Trail
——— Highways
Bodies of water
City limits
P Parking

SCALE: 1" = 0.53 MILES

US 250

Moundsville

OH 7

Ohio River

OHIO

P

12th St.

WV 2

WEST VIRGINIA

Length: 3.4 miles
Surface: Asphalt
Allowed Uses: H, B, S, A
County: Marshall
Endpoints: Glen Dale City Park (7th & S. Park Avenue) and Moundsville Riverview Park (13th Street)
Access Points: Glen Dale F/W, Moundsville F/W
Note: Follows Ohio River
Contact: Doug Paisley 304-843-4006, dpaisley@dot.state.wv.us
Trail Roughness: ★
Scenery: ★★

Directions:

From Charleston, WV: Take I-77 North to Exit 179 for WV 2. Turn right on WV 2 North and take all the way to Moundsville or Glen Dale. In Glen Dale the trailhead is near the downtown children's playground; parking is available.

In Moundsville the trailhead is at the city park; take WV 2 down or up the Ohio River, then find First Street in Moundsville. Go one mile, look for signs and follow to Moundsville Riverview Park. The trailhead is easy to find once you get to the barn on top of the hill. Parking is available.

From Columbus, OH: Take I-70 East, then a slight right to I-470 East. Enter West Virginia and take Exit 1, US 250/ WV 2 toward Wheeling. Go about 7-8 miles on WV 2 North to Glen Dale. In Glen Dale the trailhead is near the downtown children's playground; parking is available.

In Moundsville the trailhead is at the city park; take WV 2 down or up the Ohio River, then find First Street in Moundsville. Go one mile, look for signs and follow to Moundsville Riverview Park. The trailhead is easy to find once you get to the barn on top of the hill. Parking is available.

From Pittsburgh, PA: Take I-79 South to Washington, PA. Take Exit 38 onto I-70 West. Take a slight left onto I-470 West (towards Columbus). Take Exit 1, US 250/ WV 2 North. Take WV 2 North to Moundsville or on to Glen Dale. In Glen Dale the trailhead is near the downtown children's playground; parking is available.

In Moundsville the trailhead is at the city park; take WV 2 down or up the Ohio River, then find First Street in Moundsville. Go one mile, look for signs and follow to Moundsville Riverview Park. The trailhead is easy to find once you get to the barn on top of the hill. Parking is available.

WHERE TO STAY AND DINE:

Moundsville Plaza Motel
1402 Lafayette Avenue
Moundsville, WV 26041
304-845-9650

Kick Back Cafe
409 Jefferson Avenue
Moundsville, WV 26041
304-843-0055

Cheers Restaurant
325 Jefferson Avenue
Moundsville, WV 26041
304-845-4705

OTHER:

Former WV Penitentiary
818 Jefferson Avenue
Moundsville, WV 26041
304-845-6200

6. EAST WETZEL RAIL TRAIL

This trail starts in the small town of Hundred, population around 350. We were told by locals that the town was named for Henry Church and his wife, the first settlers who lived to be 109 and 106 respectively. Locals say that Henry would sit on a rocking chair on his porch near the train station. As the train came into the station, people would point and say "There's old Hundred." The name caught on, and the town became known as Hundred.

The rail trail is simply delightful and worth the trip to the bottom of the Northern Panhandle. The quaint village is out of a storybook, and the townspeople are very proud of the 1.5-mile trail. In fact, while we were riding the well-groomed, paved trail, we came across a couple of men constructing a shelter at the trailhead.

Active volunteer Barbara Brasher (below) told me at the time of publication that this shelter, which was made to look like an old railroad depot, is now completed. You will see it at the trailhead, directly across from Hundred High School. Volunteers also built two benches and an

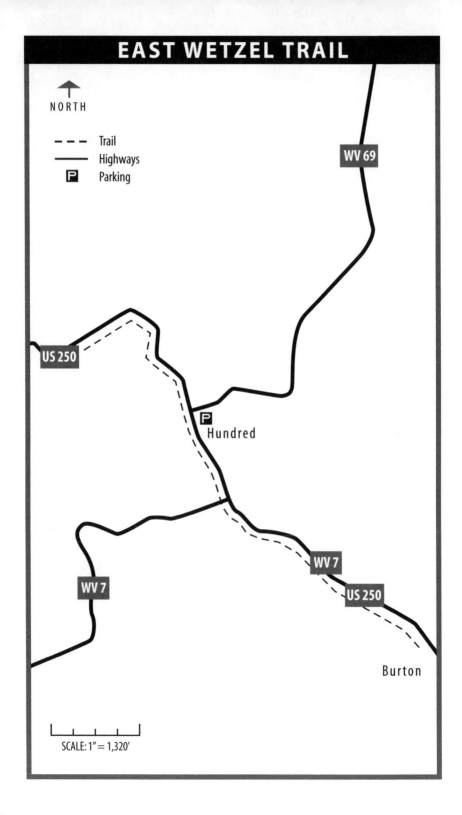

enclosed "trail update" board at this site. The trail also now boasts dusk-dawn lights. High school students walk to school on the trail, and many locals walk the trail to run errands. Within the 1.5 miles you will see the post office, the library, a bank, a Dairy Dream restaurant, some houses and some wooded sections. Bordered by Fish Creek, the trail is owned by Consolidated Coal, which gave the town right-of-way.

Length: 1.5 miles
Surface: Asphalt
Allowed Uses: H, B, A
County: Wetzel
Endpoint: Hundred
Access Point: US 250 F/W
Contact: Barbara Brasher 304-775-5680
Trail Roughness: ★
Scenery: ★★

Directions:

From Charleston: Take I-79 to exit 132 toward Fairmont. Take US 250 West about 25 miles into the town of Hundred. You will see the trail running parallel (the southwest side) along US 250 through town. Park at the trailhead, across from Hundred High School.

WHERE TO STAY AND DINE:

Fairfield Inn & Suites by Marriott
27 Southland Drive
Fairmont, WV
304-367-9150

Corner Cafe
Main Street
Hundred, WV 26575
304-775-2007

Miss Blue's Restaurant
US 250
Hundred, WV 26575
304-775-2233

Dairy Dream
US 250
Hundred, WV 26575-0436
304-775-7852

7. MON RIVER SOUTH & NORTH

We were impressed with the well-maintained Mon River Trails, which are managed by the non-profit Mon River Trails Conservancy. While riding this river valley trail the day after a storm, we saw crews working on the trail, clearing trees with a backhoe. Both north and south sections of the trail, which run alongside the Monongahela, are nice laid back, "lazy river" rides, gently curving along with bends in the river. As one continuous trail network, the Mon River Trail South and North are split by the paved Caperton Trail, which runs through Star City and Morgantown.

These trails are remote and beautiful, and with a compacted lime surface, they lose the urban feel and amenities of the paved Caperton Trail, so make sure you pack water and a snack. For the nature lover, these trails are thick with wildflowers and home to a wide variety of birds. The forests and river bottomland draw indigo buntings, goldfinches and many species of warblers as well as waterfowl and wading birds.

The north-flowing Monongahela River, thought to have been named by the Delaware Indians, means "river with sliding banks." Railroad companies took advantage of this fairly flat terrain to connect West Virginia natural resources to Pittsburgh markets. Formerly part of the Fairmont, Morgantown and Pittsburgh Railroad (and later the B & O Railroad), the trail was once the region's busiest rail line, transporting coal and coke, glass, limestone, and sand to distant markets. It is said that the locals called this railroad "Sheepskin" because they were upset that the trains caused the sheep to scatter for miles.

On the southern route, you'll pass several locks and dams and see river barges filled with coal and limestone as they travel from Fairmont to Pittsburgh. This trail goes from Morgantown to Prickett's Fort State Park, where you can link to the Marion County MC Trail for an additional 2.5 miles toward Fairmont. At Prickett's Fort State Park, you can visit the recreated frontier fort, attend a musical concert at the outdoor amphitheater or drop a fishing line in the river. They also rent

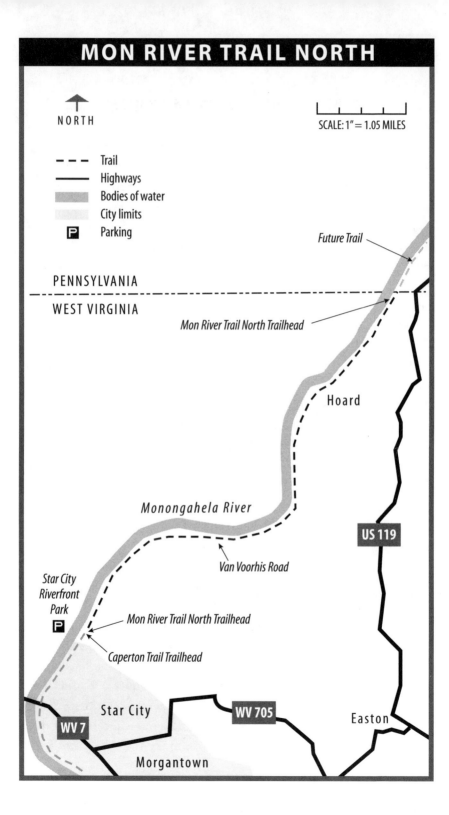

MON RIVER TRAIL NORTH

NORTH

SCALE: 1" = 1.05 MILES

- - - Trail
——— Highways
Bodies of water
City limits
P Parking

Future Trail

PENNSYLVANIA

WEST VIRGINIA

Mon River Trail North Trailhead

Hoard

Monongahela River

US 119

Van Voorhis Road

Star City
Riverfront
Park
P

Mon River Trail North Trailhead

Caperton Trail Trailhead

Star City

WV 705

Easton

WV 7

Morgantown

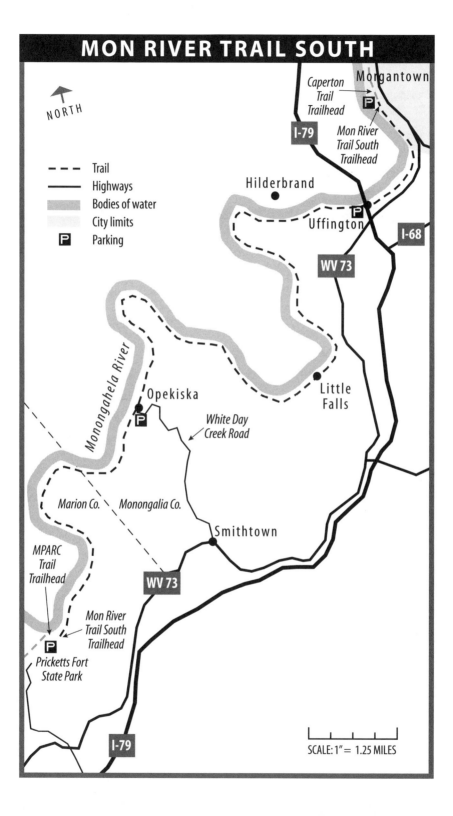

MON RIVER TRAIL SOUTH

NORTH

Trail
Highways
Bodies of water
City limits
P Parking

Morgantown

Caperton Trail Trailhead

Mon River Trail South Trailhead

I-79

Hilderbrand

Uffington

I-68

WV 73

Monongahela River

Opekiska

White Day Creek Road

Little Falls

Marion Co.   Monongalia Co.

Smithtown

MPARC Trail Trailhead

WV 73

Mon River Trail South Trailhead

Pricketts Fort State Park

I-79

SCALE: 1" = 1.25 MILES

bikes by the hour or day at the Prickett's Fort visitor center.

The six miles of trail on the north side of Morgantown, called the Mon River Trail North, also have historical and natural charms. The past history of coal mining is evident along the trail, as old coal tipples and barge-loading facilities dot the landscape. The trail currently ends at the West Virginia/Pennsylvania state line, but the plan is to continue the trail into Point Marion, Pennsylvania. Plans exist to continue the trail farther by connecting to the Cheat Lake Trail and to other Pennsylvania rail trails.

Mileage:

Mon River / Caperton Trails

0.0 WV-PA State Line
3.8 Van Voorhis Road
6.0 Pavement Starts - P
6.5 Star City Edith Barill Riverfront Park - P
8.8 Seneca Center - P

9.8 Hazel Ruby McQuain Riverfront Park - P
10.5 Mountaineer Heritage Park - P
11.7 Pavement Ends
13.3 Uffington - P
24.1 Opekiska - P
26.0 Monongalia-Marion County Line
26.4 Jordan
28.1 Catawba
29.0 Prickett's Fort State Park - P

Deckers Creek Trail

0.0 Hazel Ruby McQuain Riverfront Park - P
1.0 Valley Crossing - P
1.7 Deckers Creek Boulevard
Marilla Park - P
2.5 El Jadid & Carnegie Streets
Pavement Ends
5.9 Mellons Chapel - P

9.1 Sturgisson Chapel

10.3 Greer

11.4 Monongalia-Preston County Line

13.5 Masontown - P

15.1 Bretz Coke Ovens

16.3 Burke Road

16.9 Kingwood Pike

17.8 Reedsville- WV 92

19.0 Morgan Mine Road

Length: 17 (South), 6 (North), plus 6 miles in between the two on the Caperton Trail = 29 miles total

Surface: Crushed limestone

Allowed Uses: H, B, A

County: Marion, Monongalia

Endpoints: West Virginia/Pennsylvania state line and Prickett's Fort in Fairmont

Access Points: Van Voorhis, Star City F/W, Morgantown F/W, Uffington F/W, Opeskiska, Prickett's Fort State Park

Trail Roughness: ★★

Scenery: ★★★

Parking & Trail Access: You can order a free full-color map/ brochure of the trail from the Greater Morgantown Convention & Visitors Bureau by calling 1-800-458-7373, or email cvb@mgtn.com. The Mon River and Deckers Creek parking areas have brown directional signs at nearby roads.

Directions:

From Interstate 68: Mon River Trail North, Caperton Trail and Deckers Creek Trail: Take Exit 1, University Avenue. At the end of the ramp take a left. Follow for about two or three miles. You will pass a Go Mart gas station on your right at the top of the hill. Follow down the hill past Dorsey's Knob Park. On Southern University Avenue you will pass Waterfront Hotel on your left. Go through the light at the hotel.

Take the second left after the hotel. Bear to your right and follow down to the Wharf District parking garage.

From Interstate 68: Mon River Trail South: Take Exit 1, University Avenue. At the end of the ramp, take a left. Pass a Go Mart gas station on your right at the top of the hill. Follow down the hill past Dorsey's Knob Park. Turn left onto WV 73 and look for brown Mon River Trail signs for parking at Uffington and Opekiska Dam.

From Interstate 79: Mon River Trail South/Prickett's Fort State Park: Prickett's Fort State Park is located two miles from Interstate 79. Take Exit 139 off I-79 and look for the brown state park signs at each intersection. Follow Montana Road into the park. Prickett's Fort visitor center also rents bikes by the hour or day.

From Interstate 79: Caperton Trail and Mon River Trail North: Take Exit 155 Star City/WVU Coliseum and follow signs into Star City. After crossing the Star City Bridge turn left onto Boyers Avenue and follow signs for the Mon River Trail parking in Star City.

From Interstate 68: Deckers Creek Trail: Take Exit 4, Sabraton. Turn right off of ramp toward Morgantown and follow approximately a mile to trailhead parking at Marilla Park. Look for brown Deckers Creek Trail signs at intersection of Deckers Creek Blvd. near parking area.

WHERE TO STAY AND DINE:

Hotels, Restaurants, Bike Service in walking distance to the Mon River/Caperton/ Deckers Creek Trails:

Best Western Mountaineer Inn (Star City)
366 Boyers Avenue
Morgantown, WV 26505
304-599-5399

Springhill Suites Marriott (Sabraton)
1910 Hunters Way
Morgantown, W 26505
304-225-5200

Historic Hotel Morgan (Morgantown)
127 High Street
Morgantown, WV 26505
304-292-8200

Waterfront Place Hotel (Morgantown)
2 Waterfront Place
Morgantown, WV 26505
304-296-1700

Black Bean Burritos
132 Pleasant Street
Morgantown, WV 26505
304-296-8696

The Morgantown Brewing Company
1291 University Avenue
Morgantown, WV 26505
304-296-BREW

Maxwell's
1 Wall Street
Morgantown, WV 26505
304-292-0982

Bike Rental/Repair:
Wamsley Cycles
Located in Seneca Center beside the Caperton Trail
304-296-2447

OTHER:

Coopers Rock State Forest
61 County Line Drive
Bruceton Mills WV 26525
304-594-1561

Forks of Cheat Winery
2811 Stewartstown Road
Morgantown, WV 26508
304-598-2019

Arthurdale Heritage Museum
WV 92 (16 miles southeast of town)
Arthurdale, WV 26520
304-864-3959

8. CAPERTON RAIL TRAIL

Named for former Governor Gaston Caperton, this trail is actually the middle section of the Mon River Trail, connecting the southern and northern parts. While serving as a connector to the extensive Mon River Trail, it can stand on its own as a pleasant and convenient paved, urban trail.

This trail, paralleling the Monongahela River, skirts the edge of WVU and runs through the heart of Morgantown and the neighboring Star City. Starting in the easily accessible wharf district of Morgantown, this trail makes a perfect detour for some outdoor exercise on a West Virginia University game weekend. Parking areas to access the trail can be found at South University Park, Hazel Ruby McQuain Riverfront Park and at the Wharf District parking garage.

Morgantown was named the third-best small city in the US in a rating guide published by Prometheus Books. In addition to the university, the town is also the hub of a large arts community and offers 12,000 acres of forest at nearby Coopers Rock. We rode this trail with

a friend and his toddlers, which he pulled behind him on a trailer bike. It was the perfect length for young kids and ended at Edith Barrell Park, complete with picnic tables and a great playground for the youngsters.

There are restaurants along the trail, antique shopping at the Seneca Center, and the trail cuts through the WVU Core Arboretum. Hazel Ruby McQuain Park's outdoor amphitheater is often the center of community events including outdoor family movies and weekend festivals such as the Arts on the River

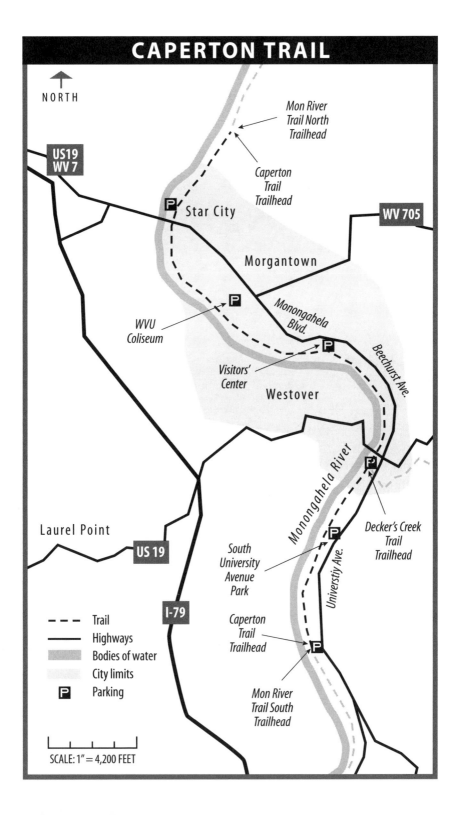

CAPERTON TRAIL

NORTH

US19
WV 7

P Star City

Mon River
Trail North
Trailhead

Caperton
Trail
Trailhead

WV 705

Morgantown

P

WVU
Coliseum

Monongahela
Blvd.

P

Visitors'
Center

Beechurst Ave.

Westover

Monongahela River

P

Decker's Creek
Trail
Trailhead

Laurel Point

US 19

P

South
University
Avenue
Park

University Ave.

I-79

Caperton
Trail
Trailhead

P

Mon River
Trail South
Trailhead

- - - Trail
——— Highways
▓▓▓ Bodies of water
░░░ City limits
P Parking

SCALE: 1" = 4,200 FEET

Festival, Mason-Dixon Festival and Labor Day festivities. Trail maps and a calendar of summer events are available at the Greater Morgantown Convention & Visitors Bureau.

Length: 6 miles
Surface: Asphalt
Allowed Uses: H, B, S, A
Counties: Monongalia
End Points: Wharf in downtown Morgantown & Star City
Access Points: Main Street, Morgantown F/W, Star City F/W
Contacts: Ralph LaRue 304-296-8356, www.boparc.com,
    info@boparc.org
Trail Roughness: ★
Scenery: ★★

(See Chapter 7 on Mon River South & North, page 27 for directions and mileage chart, as well as where to stay and dine.)

9. DECKERS CREEK TRAIL

Originally named the Morgantown & Kingwood Railroad when it was completed in 1905, (and later the B & O Railroad), today Decker's Creek trail is one of our favorites. If ridden east to west as we did from Reedsville to Morgantown, it is mostly downhill—with an 1,800-foot descent. The trail begins at Morgan Mine Road at mile 19 of the trail just outside of Reedsville. The only uphill part when riding in this direction lies at the beginning of the ride in Reedsville, where the farmland is fairly flat.

In Reedsville you should plan to check out the Arthurdale Heritage District Museum, which is recognized as the nation's first New Deal Homestead Community. The museum is a mile from the Reedsville Trailhead (mile 17.8) on WV 92. Along the way you'll see the Bretz Coke Ovens, which are listed as a National Historic Landmark and are likely to be restored in the future.

At mile 9, you'll find Dave's Snack Shop. In the trailside snack booth, you'll find Dave, a local who loves nothing more than to converse with

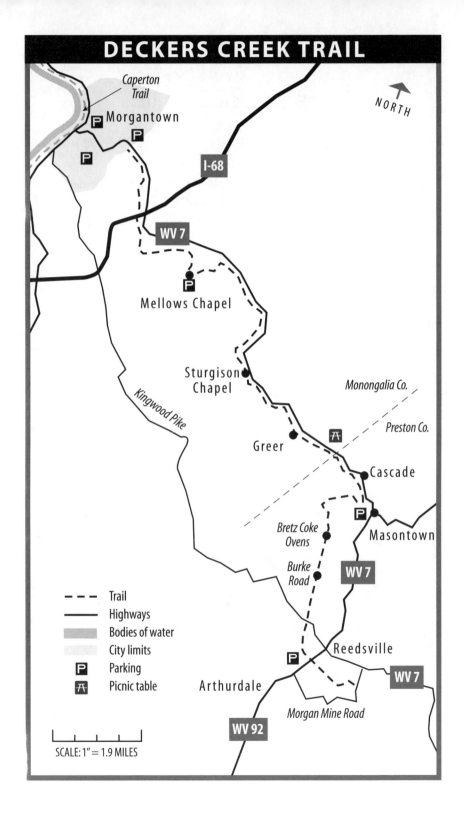

DECKERS CREEK TRAIL

Caperton Trail

Morgantown

NORTH

I-68

WV 7

Mellows Chapel

Sturgison Chapel

Kingwood Pike

Greer

Monongalia Co.

Preston Co.

Cascade

Masontown

Bretz Coke Ovens

Burke Road

WV 7

Reedsville

Arthurdale

WV 7

Morgan Mine Road

WV 92

- - - Trail
——— Highways
▨ Bodies of water
▨ City limits
🅿 Parking
🛆 Picnic table

SCALE: 1″ = 1.9 MILES

passersby. You might have to wake him up, as we did! He is a delight to talk to and certainly one of the most interesting characters on the trails. The trail is crushed limestone, but is in such good condition you will feel as if you are riding on asphalt. The trail winds down the hill through hemlock groves, hardwood forests, some marshlands and past several small waterfalls. Sightings from trail users often include white tail deer, groundhogs, beaver, the occasional bear, and a wide diversity of birds.

The trail parallels Deckers Creek, a favorite among experienced kayakers because of its class VI rapids. You may also see rock climbers on the nearby rock formations. The last stretch in Morgantown city limits becomes an urban paved trail as it cuts behind fast-food businesses and shops. There are several trail connections to city parks on this stretch: a pedestrian-bike bridge that connects to Marilla Park and access to a small dog park near mile 1. At mile 0, the trail joins the Mon River/Caperton Trails at Hazel Ruby McQuain Riverfront Park in Morgantown.

Mileage:

Mon River / Caperton Trails

0.0 WV-PA State Line
3.8 Van Voorhis Road
6.0 Pavement Starts - P
6.5 Star City Edith Barill Riverfront Park - P
8.8 Seneca Center - P
9.8 Hazel Ruby McQuain Riverfront Park - P
10.5 Mountaineer Heritage Park - P
11.7 Pavement Ends
13.3 Uffington - P
24.1 Opekiska - P
26.0 Monongalia-Marion County Line
26.4 Jordan
28.1 Catawba
29.0 Prickett's Fort State Park - P

Deckers Creek Trail

0.0 Hazel Ruby McQuain Riverfront Park - P
1.0 Valley Crossing - P
1.7 Deckers Creek Boulevard
    Marilla Park - P
2.5 El Jadid & Carnegie Streets
    Pavement Ends
5.9 Mellons Chapel - P
9.1 Sturgisson Chapel
10.3 Greer
11.4 Monongalia-Preston County Line
13.5 Masontown - P
15.1 Bretz Coke Ovens
16.3 Burke Road
16.9 Kingwood Pike

17.8 Reedsville - WV 92
19.0 Morgan Mine Road

Length: 19 miles
Surface: Asphalt, crushed limestone
Allowed uses: H, B, S (asphalt section only), A (asphalt section only)
Counties: Monongalia, Preston
End Points: Downtown wharf at Hazel Ruby McQuain Riverfront Park in Morgantown to Morgan Mine Road in the outskirts of Reedsville
Access Points: Morgantown F/W, Marilla Park, Mellons Chapel, Masontown, Reedsville
Trail Roughness: **
Scenery: ***

(See Chapter 7 on Mon River South & North, page 27 for directions and where to stay and dine.)

10. CHEAT RIVER RAIL TRAIL

One of West Virginia's best-kept secrets, this gem of a rail trail wraps around and crosses the magnificent Cheat Lake, starting at the Lake Lynn Dam and ending at the Cheat Haven Nature viewing area. The trail's construction was somewhat controversial and was publicly protested by some Cheat Lake homeowners. Eventually constructed, the secluded rail trail, which is part of a 46-acre park, is surrounded by rock faces, wooded forest and, of course, stunning lake vistas.

The only access and parking for this trail is at the end of Morgan Run Road, in the middle of the trail. From the trailhead, it is about 1 mile to the northern end of the trail at the state line, and about 4 miles to the southern end of the trail.

We found the ride across the lake's bridge to be the highlight of the ride, reminding us that Cheat Lake is truly one of the most beautiful spots in the state. The 12-foot wide, handicap-accessible trail follows the lake shoreline along an abandoned railroad right-of-way leading to

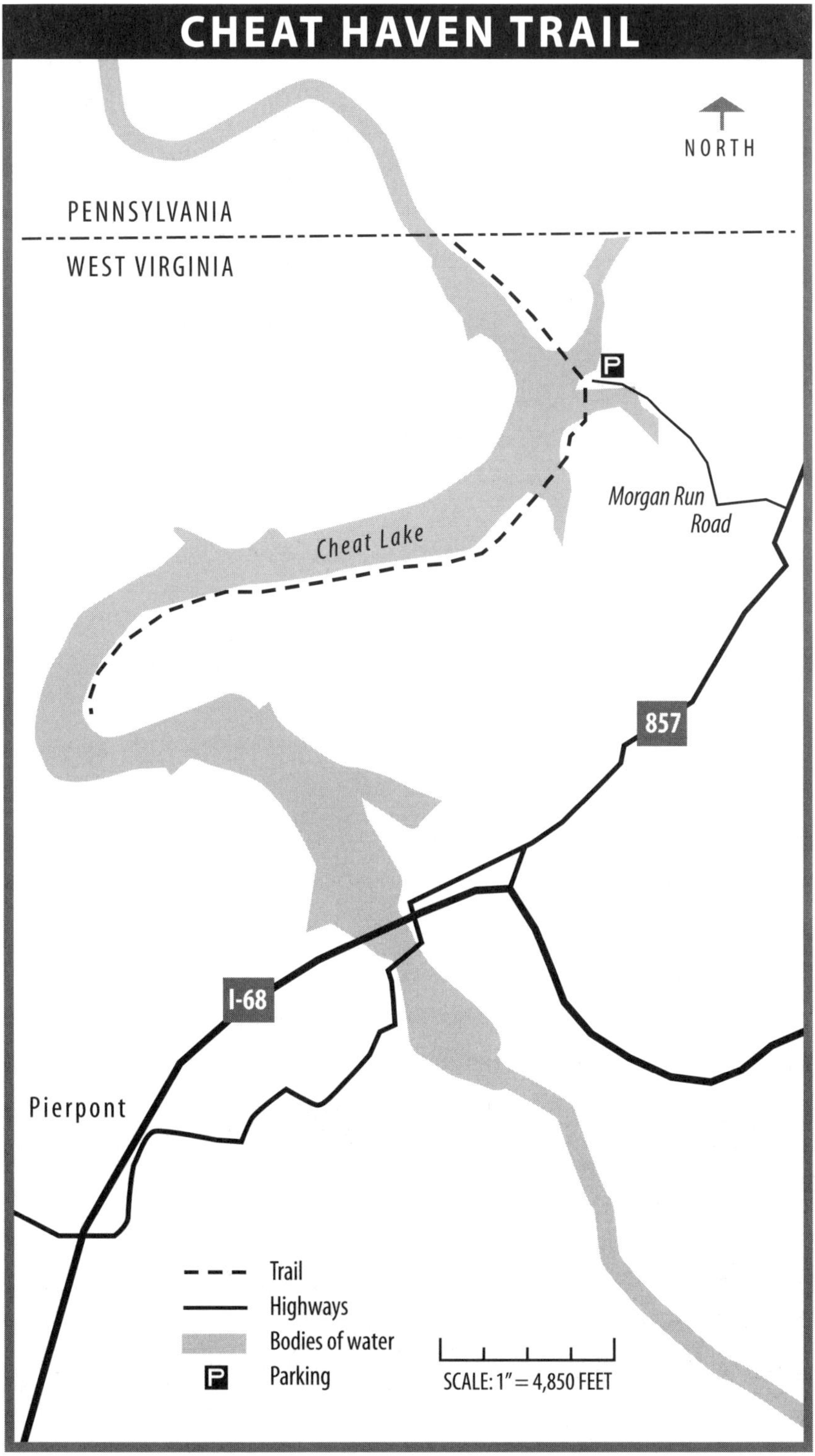

CHEAT HAVEN TRAIL

NORTH

PENNSYLVANIA

WEST VIRGINIA

Morgan Run
Road

Cheat Lake

857

I-68

Pierpont

- - - Trail
——— Highways
Bodies of water
P Parking

SCALE: 1" = 4,850 FEET

a nature viewing area at the southern tip and a fishing platform near the station at the northern tip.

The 13-mile lake was formed in 1925 by damming the Cheat River to meet the hydroelectric needs of Allegheny Energy, which maintain the lake and rail trail. The park has a children's play area, picnic sites, day-use boat docking, and camping facilities. Fishing access and car-top boat launching is situated between Rubles Run and Morgan's Run.

This southern part of the trail use to be closed for winter, but is now open year-round, subject to safe conditions concerning snow and ice. The trail is owned by Allegheny Energy and is under license with the Federal Energy Regulatory Commission as a public facility.

Length: 5.0 miles
Surface: Packed sand
Allowed Uses: H, B, A
County: Monongalia
Endpoints: Cheat Lake (Lake Lynn) Dam and Cheat Haven nature viewing area
Access Points: Near I-68, Exit 10 (F/W in nearby city of Morgantown)

Contact: Monongalia County Sheriff Trail Headquarters
304-594-2817
Trail Roughness: ★★
Scenery: ★★★★

Directions:

From Morgantown, WV: Take the Cheat Lake exit from US I-68. Turn left on WV 857 to Morgan Run Road, and then turn left onto Morgan Run Road. It is a very narrow road that becomes a one-lane road in some locations. Watch for the one-lane bridge. Morgan Run Road ends at Cheat Lake.

(See Chapter 7 on Mon River South & North, page 27 for where to stay and dine.)

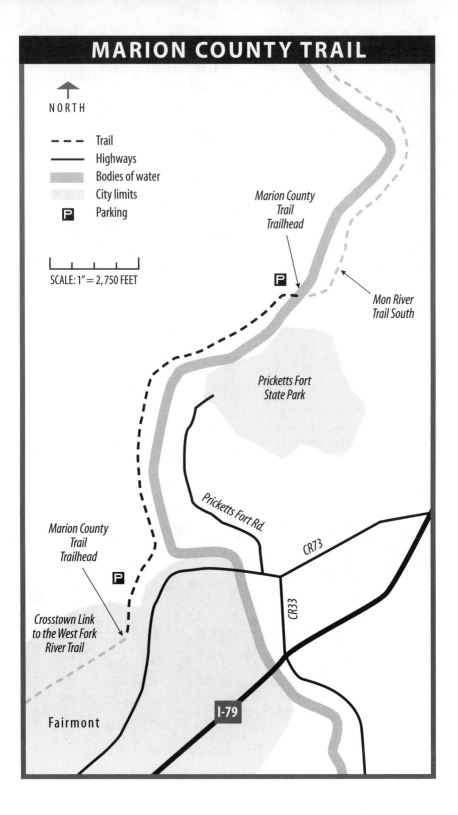

11. MARION COUNTY TRAIL (MCTRAIL)

This delightful trail starts at historic Prickett's Fort State Park, where you can see a re-creation of the 1774 fort used by colonists as a haven from Indian attacks. The fort has 16 cabins and 12-foot-high log walls. The recently paved trail also features the lighted 1,200 foot Meredith Tunnel about two miles into the ride. We found the lights especially nice after struggling to make our way through several dark-as-night tunnels on other trails. This peaceful, tree-lined trail, which runs along Prickett's Creek through rural Marion County, ends in downtown Fairmont, where there are ample opportunities for lodging and dining.

This was the first rail trail in North Central West Virginia. In 1989, the Marion County Parks and Recreation Commission (MCPARC) took ownership of 125 acres of Monongahela Railroad property. The trail was completed from Prickett's Fort State Park to the corner of Winfield Street and Morgantown Avenue in 1993. The Meredith Tunnel has been restored to its original condition of 1914. The southern trailhead was completed in 2004 and the northern trailhead was completed in 2008, with most of the work done by the MCPARC staff.

The MCTrail adjoins the Mon River Trail at Prickett's Fort State Park. With a cross-town link in Fairmont it links to the West Fork River Trail to the south. This system of trails allows riders to travel north from Shinnston, through Fairmont, up to Morgantown and the state line fairly seamlessly.

The cross-town link between Prickett's Fort and the West Fork River trail follows Mary Lou Retton Drive and Country Club Road to Fairmont Avenue

across the Monongahela River and down Morgantown Avenue to the MCTRAIL Trailhead. There are signs to show the way.

Length: 2.5 miles
Surface: Paved
Allowed Uses: H, B, A, S
County: Marion
Endpoints: Prickett's Fort State Park and Winfield Street in East Fairmont
Access Points: Fairmont F/W, Shinnston F/W
Note: Links to Mon River Trail. Lighted tunnel.
Contact: Dan Talbott 304-363-7037, mcparcfun@aol.com,
   www.mcparc.com
Trail Roughness: ★
Scenery: ★★

Directions:

To Pricketts Fort Trailhead: From Charleston, WV take I-79 North to Exit 139. Go left .5 mile to intersection of CR 73. After 1/10 a mile, go right on CR 72 and follow 2 miles to Pricketts Fork State Park. Enter park and go .25 miles to trailhead on left. Parking available.

To Morgantown Avenue (Winfield Street): From Charleston, WV: Take I-79 North, Exit 137. Go left on WV 310/Grafton Road. Follow Grafton Road onto Speedway Avenue Then turn left on Freedom Street, then right onto Union Avenue, then left onto Amos Street. Another quick turn to the right to Morgantown Avenue, then take the first road to the right, go about 1/10th a mile. Parking available.

WHERE TO STAY AND DINE:

Comfort Inn & Suites
1185 Airport Road
Fairmont, WV 26554
304-367-1370/1-800-228-5150

Days Inn
166 Middletown Road
Fairmont, WV 26554
304-366-5995

Fairfield Inn & Suites
27 Southland Drive
Fairmont, WV 26554
304-367-9150

Gillum House
35 Walnut Street
Shinnston, WV 26431
304-592-0177

Holiday Inn
930 East Grafton Road
Fairmont, WV 26554
304-366-5500 or 800-448-2296

Red Roof Inn
50 Middletown Road
Fairmont, WV 26554
304-366-6800

Super 8 Motel
2208 Pleasant Valley Road
Fairmont, WV 26554
304-363-1488

Aquarium Restaurant & Lounge
620 Gaston Avenue
Fairmont, WV 26554
304-366-1500

Aunt Baby's Soul Food
500 Pennsylvania Avenue
Fairmont, WV 26554
304-333-7685

Backwoods Grill
422 Marion Square
Fairmont, WV 26554
304-363-6533

Classics Café
236 Adams Street
Fairmont, WV 26554
304-366-3979

Colasessano's Pizza
506 Pennsylvania Avenue
Fairmont, WV 26554
304-363-9713

DJ's 50's & 60's Diner
1181 Airport Road
Fairmont, WV 26554
304-366-8110

Marie's Fine Dining & Lounge
1523 Mary Lou Retton Drive
Fairmont, WV 26554
304-366-5809

Muriale's Restaurant
1742 Fairmont Avenue
Fairmont, WV 26554
304-363-3190

Serenity Café
323 ½ Adams Street
Fairmont, WV 26554
304-816-4575

12. NORTH MARION RAIL TRAIL/ JOEL McCANN MEMORIAL TRAIL

One of the state's newest trails, the 4-mile Joel McCann Memorial Trail, runs through the heart of Mannington and features a historic train depot and many historic houses. The trail is named in honor of former fire chief Joel McCann who died in a 2002 car accident. The trail begins in nostalgic downtown Mannington, where you'll ride past red and green brick buildings along a tree-lined street with old-time lampposts and eventually past the firehouse, where a fire truck is often parked along the trail.

Keep your eye out for the magnificent George W. Bowers Estate, an 1869 Queen Anne Victorian mansion, once owned by Sen. George W. Bowers. Eventually the trail enters a woodsy area as it meanders just

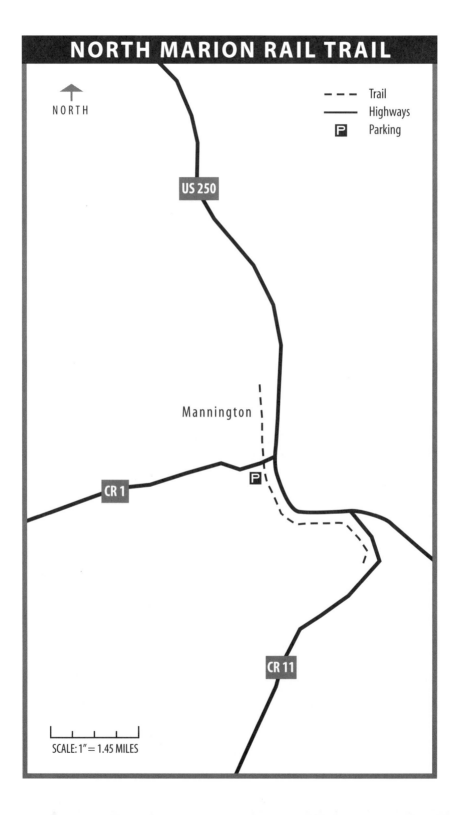

NORTH MARION RAIL TRAIL

NORTH

- - - - Trail
—— Highways
P Parking

US 250

Mannington

P

CR 1

CR 11

SCALE: 1" = 1.45 MILES

outside of town. The trail ends at the Mannington Senior Center, where plenty of good parking is available.

Length: 4 miles
Surface: Gravel
Allowed Uses: H, B
County: Marion
Endpoints: Mannington Senior Center
Access Points: Downtown Mannington
Contact: Mannington Main Street 304-986-2037
Trail Roughness: ★★★
Scenery: ★★

Directions:

From Charleston, WV: Take I-79 North to Exit 132. Go toward Fairmont, following US 250 North. Go through Fairmont and on to Mannington on US 250 North. Park anywhere downtown in Mannington.

(See Chapter 11 on Marion County Trail (McTrail), page 49 for where to stay and dine.)

13. WEST FORK RIVER RAIL TRAIL
(RALPH S. LARUE TRAIL)

The 14-mile trail (9 miles paved, 5 miles packed sand) runs along the beautiful West Fork River and past cool, copper-stained rock formations. The southern 5 miles of the trail up to the Marion County line is unpaved, the northern 9 miles in Harrison County are paved. The trail runs from Fairmont in the north, to Shinnston in the south. The trail can be connected via the across-town link in Fairmont to the McTrail, then the Mon River South and North trails.

This trail features three bridges and passes through several city parks and coal towns, the most famous being Monongah, which is the site of the December 6, 1907 mine disaster.

Shortly after Monongah, a one-mile spur off to the right takes you to Mary Lou Retton Park, named for the Fairmont native who won Olympic Gold in gymnastics in 1984. If you decide to visit this attraction, be warned that the road is a steep narrow road with no shoulder and a fair amount of traffic. Here you can turn around and return for an epic 28-mile day, or arrange for a shuttle to pick you up. If you have time, the trail continues a bit past Mary Lou Retton Park, leading to a wonderful narrow steel and wooden bridge.

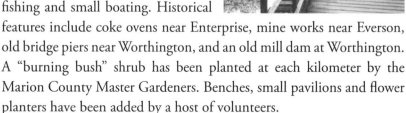

The West Fork River is popular for fishing and small boating. Historical features include coke ovens near Enterprise, mine works near Everson, old bridge piers near Worthington, and an old mill dam at Worthington. A "burning bush" shrub has been planted at each kilometer by the Marion County Master Gardeners. Benches, small pavilions and flower planters have been added by a host of volunteers.

This ride should include a stay at the Gillum House, a lovely bed

WEST FORK RIVER TRAIL
RALPH S. LARUE TRAIL

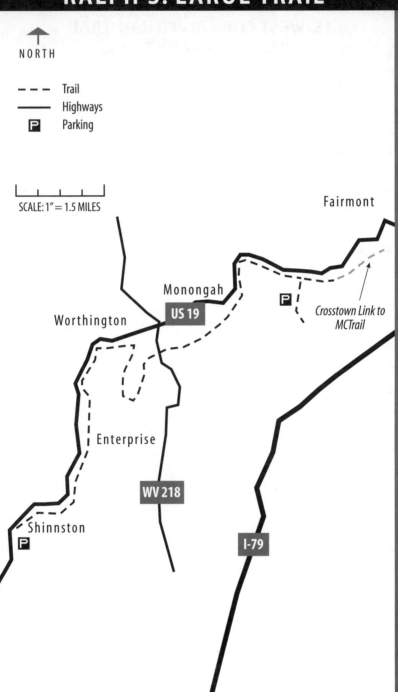

NORTH

- - - Trail
——— Highways
P Parking

SCALE: 1″ = 1.5 MILES

Fairmont

Monongah

US 19

Worthington

P

Crosstown Link to
MCTrail

Enterprise

WV 218

Shinnston

P

I-79

& breakfast with a big country porch, located 50 feet from the trail, 4 blocks from the southern trailhead, off of US 19 in Shinnston. Here you can rest up in a comfortable room and fuel up with a good old-fashioned breakfast.

In 1860 the B & O Railroad Company acquired the corridor and developed the train track in 1890. The trail, formerly owned by the B & O Railroad, was the site of a bad coal train wreck that killed an engineer in 1988.

In July of 1995, the Marion County Parks and Recreation Commission (MCPARC) acquired the track area between Shinnston and Fairmont. Trail work began in the winter of 1995. The trail opened in 1997 while improvements continued. In 1999 the Marion County Commission added the name, Ralph S. LaRue Trail, in honor of the MCPARC director responsible for the development.

Here is mileage from the traffic light in Shinnston to access points:

To Enterprise - 3.0 miles

To Hutchinson - 4.5 miles

To Everson (top of Swisher Hill coming out of Worthington) -
   6.5 miles to turn then .5 to the trail

To Monongah - 8.1 miles (turn at the school)

To Country Club Road - (turning right at the light from
   US Rt 19) 11.4 miles

To Country Club Plaza (turn right into Plaza) - 11.5 miles

Length: 14 miles

Surface: Asphalt, Packed sand

Allowed uses: E (only on shoulder edge; dismount for bridges), B, H,
   X

County: Harrison, Marion

Endpoints: Shinnston and Fairmont

Access Points: Shinnston F/W, Worthington F/W, Fairmont F/W, Everson, Monogah, Norway, Enterprise, Hutchinson
Contact: Gillum House 304-592-0177, www.shinnstonwv.com
Trail Roughness: ★★
Scenery: ★★★

(See Chapter 11 on Marion County Trail (McTrail), page 49 for where to stay and dine.)

Directions from Charleston, WV:
  To Shinnston trailhead: From I-79 North, take Exit 125 (Shinnston/Saltwell Road). Turn left and go about 1/4 a mile to Saltwell Road/WV 131. Turn left and follow WV 131 about 7 miles to US 19 in Shinnston. Turn left and the trailhead is located directly across from the Rite-Aid.
  To Enterprise trailhead: From I-79 North, take Exit 125 (Shinnston/Saltwell Road). Turn left and go about 1/4 a mile to Saltwell Road/WV 131. Turn left and follow WV 131 about 7 miles to US 19 in Shinnston. Turn right onto US 19 North. Go about 2 miles to

Enterprise. In Enterprise, watch for the right turn back (east) across the West Fork River. Turn right across the bridge, and then turn right at the end of the bridge. Park under the bridge. Facing the river, right to go north to Fairmont, left to go south to Shinnston.

To Worthington trailhead: From I-79 North, take Exit 125 (Shinnston/Saltwell Road). Turn left and go about 1/4 a mile to Saltwell Road/WV 131. Turn left and follow WV 131 about 7 miles to US 19 in Shinnston. Turn right onto US 19 North and go about 5 miles to Worthington. In Worthington, watch for the right turn back (east) across the West Fork River. Turn right and cross the bridge, then turn right into Worthington Park. There are restroom facilities at Worthington Park. The trail is at the top of the park entrance. Cross the road to enter the trail north to Fairmont. Turn hard right to go south to Shinnston.

To Monongah trailhead: From I-79 North, take Exit 125 (Shinnston/ Saltwell Road). Turn left and go about 1/4 a mile to Saltwell Road/WV 131. Turn left and follow WV 131 about 7 miles to US 19 in Shinnston. Turn right onto US 19 North. Go about 7 miles to Monongah. Turn right at the Monongah Middle School. Turn left at the stop sign. There is a large parking lot adjoining the trail. Restroom facilities.

To Fairmont trailhead: From I-79 Exit 132, go north on US 250. At the traffic light at Country Club Road and US 250 turn left onto Country Club Road (Giant Eagle is to the right). Proceed on Country Club Road and turn left into the shopping plaza (approximately 1 1/2 mile). To the left of the Fairmont Credit Union is Edgeway Street, a dead end. Go down Edgeway to a farm gate on the right just before the street ends. Go around the gate. WALK your bike down the lift station road to the right-of-way at the bottom. The trail surface is a bit rough for about 1 mile to the official rail trail start.

To Everson trailhead: From Monongah trailhead. Turn right on County Road 56. Go .5 mile to intersection of US 19, then turn left. Go 1.5 miles to County Road 27. Turn left and travel .5 mile to Everson Bridge. Trailhead is on right past bridge.

To Hutchinson trailhead: From junction of WV 131 and US 19, turn right and drive north. Turn right onto the first bridge after entering Marion County to Hutchinson. Go 2/10 mile to Hutchinson Park and trailhead on left.

14. HARRISON COUNTY HIKE AND BIKE RAIL TRAIL

While a little more rugged than the Harrison County Southern Rail Trail (see page 84), this route offers about seven miles of flat, scenic riding. You'll enter the southern end of the trail just off of US 50. Upon first entering the trail, check out the bright blue and green rail trail mural that was created by Americorps. We found this trail to be quite rough in spots and not maintained as well as some others, but it's worth the ride/hike as you follow the winding West Fork River through heavily wooded areas thick with trees and streams.

Though the trail connects Clarksburg to Spelter, the trail is now closed from the Rolland Glass Plant site to the end of the trail in Spelter. The WV DEP has performed preliminary testing and closed this section of the trail until allegations of toxic waste contamination is resolved. Signs have been posted along the trail. Please be safe and not ride this section of the trail.

You can, however, make a trip to the Rolland Glass Plant in the neighborhood of North View to the Dupont property, where you can turn around and ride back for a full afternoon's riding, or arrange for a shuttle to pick you up.

Length: 7 miles, once trail re-opens to Spelter
Surface: Cinders
Allowed uses: H, B, E, X
County: Harrison
Endpoints: Clarksburg
Access points: Clarksburg F/W,
Note: Follows West Fork River

HARRISON COUNTY
HIKE AND BIKE RAIL TRAIL

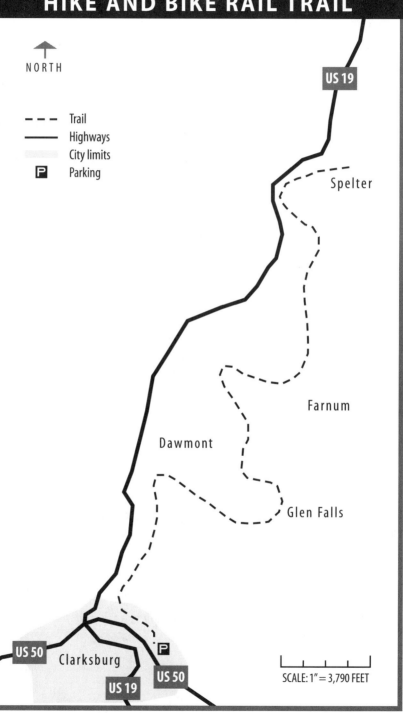

NORTH

- - - Trail
——— Highways
City limits
P Parking

US 19

Spelter

Farnum

Dawmont

Glen Falls

US 50

Clarksburg

P

US 50

US 19

US 50

SCALE: 1" = 3,790 FEET

Contact: Harrison County Parks & Recreation 304-624-8619,
    kmcallum@harrisoncountywv.com

Trail Roughness: ★★

Scenery: ★★★

Directions:

From Charleston, WV: Take I-79 North to Exit 119 for Clarksburg. Go left on US 50 West. From US 50 exit to West Virginia Avenue. Turn left on West Virginia Avenue, then right on N. 19th Street, continuing until past Marino Brothers, turn left on Williams Avenue. Continue on Williams Avenue to N. 25th Street. Turn right on N 25th Street, continue on N. 25th Street to the trailhead, just before the dead end. Parking is on left, near the Rolland Glass Plant. There are signs leading to the trailhead from US 50.

To Spelter: *Please note that access to the rail trail from Spelter is temporarily prohibited at the time of this book publication.*

WHERE TO STAY AND DINE:

Towne House Motor Lodge West
US 50 West
Clarksburg, WV 26301
304-623-3716

Parkette Family Restaurant
Rt. 2, Box 405
Clarksburg, WV 26301
304-623-0155

15. NORTH BEND RAIL TRAIL

A part of the 5,500-mile coast-to-coast American Discovery Trail and covering 72 miles from Parkersburg to Wolf Summit (near Clarksburg), the North Bend Rail Trail truly is a West Virginia treasure. Richard "Dick" Bias deserves much credit for founding the trail—raising much of the $350,000 needed to purchase the trail and remaining a dedicated volunteer until his death in 1995.

The trail runs through small towns, quiet woods and farms for 72 miles from Parkersburg to Wolf Summit, roughly paralleling US 50. Now popular among hikers, bikers and horseback riders, the trail was once part of a major corridor of the Baltimore & Ohio Railroad, which was responsible for boosting the economy of many of the towns along the way. The B & O Railroad was completed in 1857; the hilly terrain and numerous creeks necessitated the building of 36 bridges and 23 tunnels—13 of which still exist and 10 of which you will pass through on the trail. The three other tunnels were abandoned but can still be seen from the trail. In 1989 the conversion from a railroad track to

NORTH BEND RAIL TRAIL

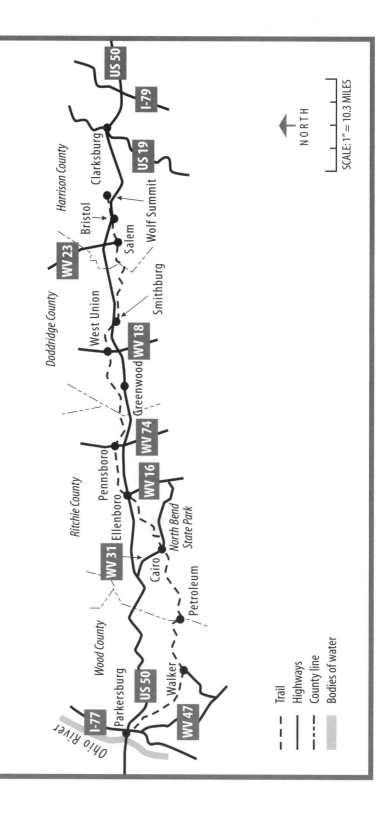

SCALE: 1" = 10.3 MILES

NORTH

Ohio River

I-77
Parkersburg
Wood County
US 50
Walker
WV 47

WV 31
Cairo
North Bend
State Park
Petroleum
Ritchie County
Ellenboro
Pennsboro
WV 16
WV 74

Greenwood
WV 18
West Union
Doddridge County
Smithburg

WV 23
Bristol
Salem
Wolf Summit
Harrison County
Clarksburg
US 19

US 50
I-79

--- Trail
--- Highways
--- County line
▨ Bodies of water

a trail was initiated by Bias. With only a 3% grade, the trail's gravel surface is ideal for recreational use.

We easily rode the entire trail over three days with our two children: me pulling our 6-year-old daughter on a trailer bike and our 10-year old on his own bike. We stayed at the lodge at North Bend State Park each night and arranged private shuttles each day to help us get between the trail and the park. (Unfortunately at this time, no public shuttles are available.)

While at the lodge, the kids enjoyed swimming and playing miniature golf. A couple of days my son and I mustered up enough energy after our trail ride to check out some of the single-track mountain bike trails near the lodge. With a top-notch restaurant and fun, relaxed atmosphere, the lodge was a perfect place to "come home to" every evening.

Each day's ride was an adventure, as we pedaled through towns and wandered in and out of little mom-and-pop shops, ate ice cream and learned a little bit of history about each place. Unlike many of the rail trails, which are all about taking you into remote parts of the state, this rail trail—while remote and incredibly scenic most of the way—also offered many interesting places to visit. I remember this rail trail as more

of a journey than a ride.

Park Superintendent Steve Jones rode several sections of the trail with us, telling us interesting tidbits about the trail's heritage. We had a lot of fun counting tunnels and anticipating when we would approach the next one. The tunnels are at mile markers 13.1, 14.1, 21.9, 28.9, 30.14, 37.3, 39.1, 49, 58.5 and 68.1. One word of warning, you will want to have a headlamp or flashlight with you on this trail; some of the tunnels are quite long and become pitch black once inside.

The most memorable part of the ride for me was the Silver Run Tunnel at mile marker 21.9. Shortly before we reached this tunnel, a storm moved in and it was raining quite hard. My husband and daughter left the trail and joined the shuttle, while my son and I ventured on. Steve had told us that this particular tunnel was haunted by a woman in a white, flowing dress; my son didn't seem to be phased by this and even seemed a bit excited about it. That is, until we reached the tunnel. The rain was beating down and the air was thick with gray fog. As we approached the tunnel, water was running fiercely off the top of the stone entranceway. All we could see was an entrance into cold blackness. I will never forget the look on his face when he said to me "I'm not going in there. I'm going back." Of course, going back wasn't an option at this

point. I finally talked him
into going into the tunnel,
but he insisted we walk—
which required us to walk
through several inches of
water. (Luckily, no ghost
sightings!)

The whole family
enjoyed trekking through
Cairo (25.1 mile marker),
where we visited Dinah's,
a shop specializing in goat
milk soaps; R.C. Marshall
Hardware, which has been
around since 1902; and Berdine's 5 & Dime, with bins of novelties, tin
toys and bulk candies. Cairo was once home to two marble factories;
today the Ritchie County Veterans Memorial stands in the town square.
This monument has a downstream panel from the dam at North Bend
State Park. When contractor Barnard Construction of Bozeman,
Montana, built the dam, they donated an extra panel, which now holds

the bronze plaques commemorating the wars and those who served.

Also in Cairo is the Historic Bank of Cairo, which is on the National Historic Register, and Country Trail Bikes, which was featured as a 2006 *Rand McNally* "Best of the Road" and Editor's Pick for their 2006 *Rand McNally Atlas*. The old-time general store at the bike shop was also named "One of 55 Good Things about West Virginia" by *The State Journal* in 2006.

The longest tunnel on the trail, Tunnel #6 is at mile marker 49, where you can find a pit toilet, camping and shelter. This tunnel is 2,297-feet long; we felt like we were riding for quite a while before we actually saw a flicker of light from the other side of the tunnel.

At mile 50.8 you'll hit West Union, which you'll access via the longest bridge on the trail over Middle Creek Island. At 53.7 miles is the town of Smithburg, with the restored Smithton Depot. There you will find a picnic area with primitive campsites. At mile marker 64.7 you'll find the old B & O Depot, which is quaintly restored and holds a vast array of memorabilia for history lovers. Beside it is a caboose, a large pavilion for picnics and a performance stage.

You'll pass a Dairy Queen and a Veterans Memorial in Salem. While here, eat at Boyd's Place. Fort New Salem is about 1.5 miles

from the trail and is an historic village portraying life in earlier times. (If you're on the trail the first weekend of October, check out the Apple Butter Festival in Salem.)

The end of your journey brings you to Wolf Summit, where you'll want to make the quick trip to Clarksburg. Stonewall Jackson was born there in 1824 and is commemorated by a statue on Main Street. The city also boasts plenty of restaurants, lodging and shopping.

Length: 72 miles
Surface: Packed gravel, packed sand, varied roughness
Allowed Uses: H, B, E
Counties: Wood, Ritchie, Doddridge, Harrison
Endpoints: Parkersburg and Wolf Summit
Access Points: Walker F/W, Petroleum F/W, Cairo F/W, Ellenboro F/W, Pennsboro F/W, Greenwood F/W, West Union F/W, Smithburg F/W, Salem F/W, Bristol F/W, Wolf Summit F/W, Parkersburg F/W
Note: 9 tunnels; part of the American Discovery Trail
Contact: North Bend State Park 304-643-2931, www.wvparks.com/northbendrailtrail, www.NorthBendRailTrail.com
Trail Roughness: ★★
Scenery: ★★★

Directions:

To western trailheads From Charleston, WV: Follow I-77 North about 75 miles to Parkersburg. Exits to trail at either WV 47 or US 50. See detailed "trailhead" directions below to each location.

To eastern trailheads From Charleston, WV: Follow I-79 North about 120 miles to Clarksburg. Exit west US 50, follow about 6 miles to first trailhead. See detailed "trailhead" directions below to each location.

From Columbus, OH: Follow I-70 east to I-77. Follow I-77 South to Parkersburg. Exits to trail at either WV 47 or US 50.

From Pittsburgh, PA: Follow I-79 South about 100 miles to Clarksburg. Exit west US 50, follow about 6 miles to first trailhead.

From Elkins, WV: Follow US 33 West about 50 miles to I-79. Turn north on I-79, follow about 20 miles to Clarksburg. Exit west US 50, follow about 6 miles to first trailhead.

The trailheads:

Parkersburg: From I-77 North, take Exit 174, turning (right) onto WV 47 and go 7/10 mile, turn right on Happy Valley Road and go 3/10 mile to rail trail. Park on right side of road; this is the Western Terminus of the NBRT.

Walker: From Parkersburg I-77 Exit 174, turn east on WV 47, turn right immediately onto old Rt. 47, go about 7 miles, turn left on Walker Road, and follow about 7 miles until crossing rail trail. Rail trail is visible from Walker Road for several miles before trailhead. Right on trail is west toward Parkersburg, left is east toward Clarksburg.

Petroleum: From US 50, exit south on Goose Creek Road, follow about 7 miles to the community of Petroleum. Park at rail trail crossing. Heading right on trail is west toward Parkersburg, left is east toward Clarksburg.

Cairo: From US 50, exit south on WV 31, follow about 4 miles across bridge in Cairo. The rail trail crosses WV 31 in the center of the business district. Parking is on left in front of bike shop, on right

after trail along WV 31, and on Sunday, in bank parking lot after trail, about 100 yards on left. If there is no parking available in Cairo, proceed on WV 31 to turn off to North Bend State Park. (Although there are several dozen parking spots in Cairo, parking can be hard to find on nice spring and fall weekends. Cairo is often the most crowded trailhead along the North Bend.)

North Bend State Park from Parkersburg: From US 50 East, exit south on WV 31, follow signs through Cairo to North Bend State Park, about 7 miles. At entrance to park, go past main lodge, following signs to the campground. At the campground, turn left across bridge into recreation area. Parking is available along road through recreation area. On bicycle or foot, follow road through recreation area to 1/2 mile access trail past picnic shelter to rail trail. At intersection of access trail and rail trail, right is east toward Clarksburg, and left is west toward Parkersburg.

North Bend State Park from Clarksburg: From US 50 West, exit south on WV 16 at Ellenboro. Follow signs through Harrisville to North Bend State Park, about 10 miles. At park entrance, go past main lodge, following signs to the campground. At the campground, turn left across bridge into recreation area. Parking available along road through recreation area. On bicycle or foot follow road through recreation area to

1/2 mile long access trail past picnic shelter to rail trail. At intersection of access trail and rail trail, right is east toward Clarksburg, and left is west toward Parkersburg.

Ellenboro: From US 50, exit north onto WV 16, parking lot 1/4 mile on right just beyond trail overpass. From parking lot, right across overpass is west toward Parkersburg, left is east toward Clarksburg. If trailhead parking lot is full, public parking is available along town streets to the east of the trail overpass.

Pennsboro: From US 50, exit north onto WV 74, go one mile to old Depot on rail trail. Facing Depot from parking lot right is east, toward Clarksburg, and left is west, toward Parkersburg.

Greenwood: From US 50, exit north at Greenwood exit, follow exit road about 1/2 mile, park at WV Dept. of Highways or at Greenwood Motel. Trail is on hillside behind motel.

West Union: From US 50, exit north onto WV 18. Cross under longest trail trestle, visible from US 50, and turn right to athletic field or left to town. Facing trail trestle from US 50, right is east toward Clarksburg, and left is west toward Parkersburg.

Smithburg: From US 50, exit south at Smithburg exit, turn right at bottom of hill onto old Rt. 50, go left on old Rt. 50 1/2 mile to Smithburg Depot and Spencer Park. Parking is available in front of

depot or at park. Facing the depot from old Rt. 50, right is west toward Parkersburg, and left is east toward Clarksburg.

Salem: From US 50, exit south onto WV 23, continue into town to depot. The trail runs the length of town. From WV 23, facing the depot, right is west toward Parkersburg and left is east toward Clarksburg.

Bristol: From US 50, exit south onto Raccoon Run Road. Raccoon Run Road crosses the trail immediately. Park alongside the trail or at the nearby bike shop. From US 50, right is west toward Parkersburg, and left is east toward Clarksburg.

Wolf Summit: From US 50, exit north at the Wolf Summit exit. Turn right and follow the road about a mile to the old school building on the right. This is known as the Dorothy Springer building. There's not much parking, but enough for a few cars. The exit crosses the trail immediately. From US 50 left is west toward Parkersburg, right is the Eastern Terminus, a few hundred feet away. Wolf Summit is the access point closest to Clarksburg.

Mileage:

Wood County Section
0.0 - Western Terminus NBRT
1.0 - Happy Valley Road

2.7 - trail crossing private campground

5.7 - trail crossing road following along River Road

6.4 - WV 47 overpass

7.3 - bridge crossing - decked

7.9 - bridge crossing - decked

9.5 - bridge crossing - decked

10.3 - bridge crossing - decked (Red brick building is Walker Post Office)

10.6 - trail crossing road

11.0 - Walker Model Section

13.1 - Tunnel #22, abandoned

13.8 - slip, proceed with caution

14.1 - Tunnel #21 (1,840'), Eaton Tunnel 2nd longest, smooth

Ritchie County Section

15.3 - gravel road crossing, Eaton Road

16.0 - gravel road crossing, Eaton Road

16.7 - Bridge 45 over Goose Creek - decked

16.8 - Bridge 44 over Goose Creek - decked

17.2 - Bridge 43 over Goose Creek - decked

17.3 - Bridge 42 over Goose Creek - decked

17.9 - Town of Petroleum (Elev. 700') camping, rest area, pit toilet, shelter and fire ring

18.0 - Bridge 41 over Goose Creek - decked Bridge 40 over Goose Creek - decked

18.8 - wetland area north of trail (ducks, Canadian Geese, turtles, etc.)

19.0 - Bridge 39 over Goose Creek - decked

19.1 - Bridge 38 over Goose Creek - decked

19.2 - Bridge 37 over Goose Creek - decked

21.9 - Tunnel #19, Silver Run Tunnel (1,376') brick, damp Take a flashlight, reported to be haunted!

22.5 - gravel road crossing Silver Run Road

25.1 - Bridge (decked) 36 over North Fork of Hughes River, WV 31 crossing Town of Cairo (elev. 678') groceries, bike shop, WV crafts

28.9 - Tunnel #12 (577') smooth and damp

30.4 - Cement bridge with steel side rails Tunnel #10 (377') Dick Bias
    Tunnel, carved from solid rock, damp Concrete bridge with side
    rails

31.3 - gravel road crossing

31.5 - Hobo Rock & Spring, north of trail

31.7 - gravel road crossing, Way Station Road

32.3 - US 50 overpass

32.4 - Ritchie County Middle/High School

33.5 - NBRT overpass of WV 16, steepest grade on trail

33.6 - Town of Ellenboro (elev. 785') food, glass and marble factories

33.4 - Bridge 27A over creek, decked & side-railed

35.2 - Bridge 27 over creek, decked & side-railed

35.3 - gravel road crossing

35.8 - gravel road crossing

36.6 - Old Rt. 50 overpass

37.0 - paved road crossing

37.3 - Tunnel #8 (588') brick

38.2 - Town of Pennsboro (elev. 861') B&O Depot being restored;
    WV 74 crossing; lodging, food and bike service

39.1 - Tunnel #7 (779') brick, Old Rt. 50 crosses over tunnel

41.1 - Bridge 26, over North Fork of Hughes River (cement with
    gravel surface and side rails)

41.7 - Town of Toll Gate (elev. 798')

Doddridge County Section

43.3 - Town of Greenwood (elev. 856') food and lodging

44.0 - paved road crossing, traffic, caution

47.6 - Town/Central Station (elev. 815')

47.9 - cement bridge with gravel surface and side rails

49.0 - Tunnel #6 (2,297') longest
    Rest Area: pit toilet, camping, shelter and fire ring added soon

49.6 - Bridge 24, over Old Rt. 50, cement with side rails

50.8 - Town of West Union (elev. 836') food and lodging

51.0 - Bridge 23 (decked and longest) over WV 18/Middle Island
    Creek

51.2 - Bridge 22 (decked) over Middle Island Creek
53.1 - Bridge 21 (decked) over Middle Island Creek
53.7 - Town of Smithburg (elev. 794') Smithton Depot (restored
       Spencer Park picnic area, five primitive campsites)
54.0 - US 50 bridge overpass
54.5 - Bridge 20 (decked) over Middle Island Creek
55.6 - Bridge 19, cement w/gravel, side rails

New Model Section
55.9 - Bridge 18 cement w/gravel, side rails
57..5 - Bridge 17 with side rails
57.7 - Long Run Road crossing Tunnel #4 (846') Long Run Tunnel
58.5 - Tunnel #3, abandoned
59.1 - Crossing - Long Run Road
59.9 - Bridge, cement w/gravel and side rails
61.4 - Crossing - Long Run Road Town of Industrial (elev. 1,075')
63.0 - Crossing - Long Run Road

Harrison County Section
64.7 - Town of Salem (elev. 1,046') B & O Depot being restored; food
       and lodging
66.8 - Rest Area: Pit toilet, shelter, camping
67.1 - Town of Bristol (elev. 1,090') primitive camping
68.1 - Tunnel #2 (1,086') damp and rough
69.1 - Bridge 14, cement w/gravel, side rails
71.0 - paved road crossing

Eastern Terminus - Wolf Summit, Clarksburg: elevation 1,136

WHERE TO STAY AND DINE:

North Bend State Park & Restaurant
Cairo, WV 26337
304-643-2931

Greenbrier Motel
200 Buckhannon Pike
Clarksburg, WV 26301
304-624-5518

Sutton Inn
250 Emily Drive
Clarksburg, WV 26301
304-623-2600

Sleep Inn
115 Tolley Drive
Bridgeport, WV 26330
304-842-1919

Jackson Square Bed & Breakfast
154 E. Main Street
Clarksburg, WV 26301
304-624-7233

Audia's Country Kitchen
301 W. Pike Street
Clarksburg, WV 26301
304-623-0202

Greenbrier Motel & Restaurant
200 Buckhannon Pike
Clarksburg, WV 26301
304-624-5518

USA Steak Buffet
101 Lodgeville Road
Clarksburg, WV 26301
304-842-3150

Washington Square
215 Washington Avenue
Clarksburg, WV 26301
304-623-6000

To determine the distance between points on the trail find your location in the top column then go down the row to the your destination point. The intersection of column & row is your mileage.

	PETROLEUM	WOLF SUMMIT	WILSONBURG	WEST UNION	WALKER	SMITHBURG	SALEM	TOLL GATE	PENNSBORO	NORTH BEND	MOUNTWOOD	ELLENBORO	CAIRO
CAIRO	7	45	46	25	14	28	39	16	13	3	9	7	
ELLENBORO	14	38	39	18	21	21	32	9	6	4	16		9
MOUNTWOOD PARK	2	54	55	34	5	37	48	25	22	12		16	3
NORTH BEND STATE PARK	10	42	43	22	17	25	32	13	10		12	4	13
PENNSBORO	20	32	33	12	27	15	26	3		10	22	6	7
PETROLEUM		52	53	32	7	35	46	23	20	10	2	14	16
TOLL GATE	23	29	30	9	30	12	23		3	13	25	9	39
SALEM	46	6	7	14	53	11		23	26	32	48	32	28
SMITHBURG	35	17	18	3	42		11	12	15	25	37	21	14
WALKER	7	59	60	39		42	53	30	27	17	5	21	25
WEST UNION	32	20	21		39	3	14	9	12	22	34	18	46
WILSONBURG	53	1		21	60	18	7	30	33	43	55	39	45
WOLF SUMMIT	52		1	20	59	17	6	29	32	42	54	38	45

16. HARRISON COUNTY SOUTHERN RAIL TRAIL

This 5-mile packed sand and crushed limestone trail takes you through West Virginia farmland, where you'll pass peaceful settings of horses grazing along fences, meadows of bright wildflowers and nostalgic wooden bridges. You'll also come across some religious slogans and CSX signage. With vast acres of farmland and old-time wooden bridges, we felt as if we'd been transported miles away from city life. The very well marked trail, which parallels the hard road at times, begins to the east just off of the Lost Creek exit from I-79 and ends in Mt. Clare. The trail becomes more and more rural as it continues to Mt. Clare.

Harrison County is preparing to improve the next 5.5 miles of trail, which ends at Wendy's at the intersection of Rt. 19 and Melford Street in Clarksburg. This section of trail will become part of the Clarksburg Park System at the Veterans Park.

Length: 5 miles
Surface: Packed sand
Allowed uses: H, B, E
County: Harrison
Endpoints: Lost Creek and Mount Clare
Access Points: Lost Creek F/W, Mount Clare F/W
Contact: Harrison County Parks & Recreation 304-624-8619
Trail Roughness: ★★
Scenery: ★★

Directions:
To Lost Creek: Take I-79 to Exit 110 toward Lost Creek and follow signs to Lost Creek. As you're headed into the village of Lost Creek,

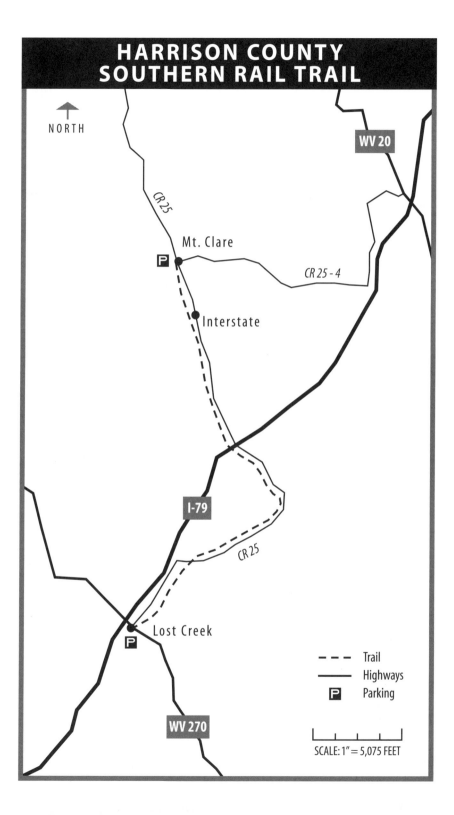

you'll see a gas station on your left and a railroad depot on your right. The trailhead is near the railroad depot. It is recommended that riders/ hikers start at the Lost Creek trailhead.

To Mt. Clare: Take I-79 to Exit 110 toward Lost Creek and follow signs to Lost Creek. In Lost Creek, take a right on CR 25, Lost Creek Road. Follow CR 25 for 5 miles, crossing under the interstate about halfway to Mt. Clare.

WHERE TO STAY AND DINE:

Plantation Inn & Suites
1322 Hackers Creek Road
Jane Lew, WV 26378
304-884-7806

Greenbrier Motel
200 Buckhannon Pike
Clarksburg, WV 26301
304-624-5518

Sutton Inn
250 Emily Drive
Clarksburg, WV 26301
304-623-2600

Sleep Inn
115 Tolley Drive
Bridgeport, WV 26330
304-842-1919

Jackson Square Bed & Breakfast
154 E. Main Street
Clarksburg, WV 26301
304-624-7233

Greenbrier Motel & Restaurant
200 Buckhannon Pike
Clarksburg, WV 26301
304-624-5518

USA Steak Buffet
101 Lodgeville Road
Clarksburg, WV 26301
304-842-3150

Jane Lew Depot
6298 Main Street
Jane Lew, WV 26378
304-884-8910

Quietdale Sports Grill
Mount Clare, WV 26408
304-624-3760

17. BARNUM RAIL TRAIL

Because of the sometimes-rough ballast surface, a sturdy mountain bike (or good hiking skills) is needed for this out-and-back trail that runs along the north branch of the Potomac River. Starting in the small community of Barnum, just north of Randolph Jennings Lake, the trailhead is essentially the only way on and off of this remote trail. We were impressed with the splendid scenery, most especially of the white water river, a popular trout fishing spot, which is quickly becoming a rafting and kayaking hot spot. The trail begins in the very small community of Barnum, just north of Randolph Jennings Lake in Mineral County. The trailhead has plenty of parking, restroom facilities, and a little park overlooking the Potomac River that offers fishing.

BARNUM RAIL TRAIL

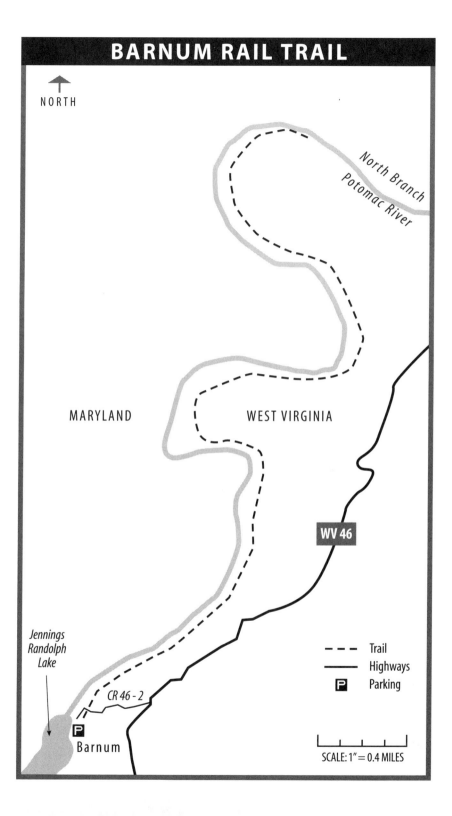

NORTH

North Branch
Potomac River

MARYLAND

WEST VIRGINIA

WV 46

Jennings
Randolph
Lake

CR 46 - 2

P

Barnum

- - - Trail
——— Highways
P Parking

SCALE: 1" = 0.4 MILES

Be very careful for the first mile; the trail is open to vehicular traffic, though we didn't see any cars during our ride. Here the trail is used for river access to Barnum Whitewater Area. You will pass a large parking area and a closed gate; the remaining three miles will be closed to motorized traffic.

After the gate, the trail heads into the open and offers stunning views of the Potomac. You will pass wooded hillsides as the trail hugs the west slope; you will see the river on your left for the next two miles. At about the halfway point, you'll see an old family-owned coalmine, marked with a wooden sign. Though there is no official signage marking the end of the trail, you'll know because the trail will not be maintained. Western Maryland Railroad laid the previous railroad track in 1919.

This is quite a remote trail with no access to water or other amenities. Make sure to bring plenty of water for the duration of your visit. Having extra supplies in the car is a good idea also.

Affordable rustic cabins can be rented alongside the trail; several outfitters offer rafting/kayaking excursions.

Length: 4.2 miles
Surface: Packed stone/varied roughness

Allowed Uses: H, Mt.B, E
County: Mineral
Endpoints: Barnum, below Jennings Randolph Dam, along North
    Branch Potomac River
Access Points: Barnum
Contact: Rex Riffle 304-788-5732, www.mineralcountywv.com
Trail Roughness: ★★★
Scenery: ★★★

Directions:

From I-68—Exit I-68 at Cumberland, MD. Take the Green Street
Exit (US 220 South). Follow US 220 South to Keyser. Turn right onto
MD 135 W/Queens Point Road SW. Follow MD 135, then turn left
onto WV 46 W. Turn right onto CR 46/2. Barnum Road. Follow
Barnum Road about 2 miles to the parking area.

From Interstate 81—Take US 50 West exit at Winchester, VA.
Follow US 50 West roughly 75 miles to WV 42 North. Turn right and
take WV 42 North to WV 46 East. Take a slight right onto WV 46 East
and follow to CR 46/2, Barnum Road. Turn left onto Barnum Road
and go about 2 miles to the parking area.

From I-79—Follow US 50 East to US 219. Turn left on US 219 North and take to Oakland, MD. In Oakland, turn right on MD 135. Follow to WV 46 and go right. Turn right onto CR 46/2/Barnum Road and follow about 2 miles to the parking area.

WHERE TO STAY AND DINE:

Keyser Inn
New Creek Drive
Keyser, WV 26726
304-788-0913

Candlewyck Inn
65 S Mineral Street
Keyser, WV 26726
304-788-6594

18. BLACKWATER CANYON TRAIL

Cyclists and hikers should take caution. The trail is not well maintained and quite dangerous in spots. The Forest Service actually does not recommend use of this trail because it is not maintained and several culverts are washing out. For experienced riders and hikers who choose to check out the trail, take care to stay on the uphill side of the grade. It's also a good idea to contact the Forest Service prior to riding this trail for updates on its condition.

We began our journey in Thomas, staying at the Fiddler's Roof Guesthouse, a small family-owned bed and breakfast, with an adjoining café, The Purple Fiddle. The latter is known for its mountain music and for having the largest beer collection in the state. Having ridden off-road, largely on single-track trails all over the Blackwater Canyon area, I was surprised to find an entire rail trail that I had never been on.

Knowing that the riding in this area is pretty technical with lots of roots and rocks, I was amazed to find a fairly smooth route that runs along the hillside above the North Fork of the Blackwater River—and for most of its length quite a ways above the river. While this provides for excellent vistas and views of the canyon, it also increases the danger of severe injury should cyclists crash into a washed-out culvert and, potentially, over the side of the route.

We rode this trail from

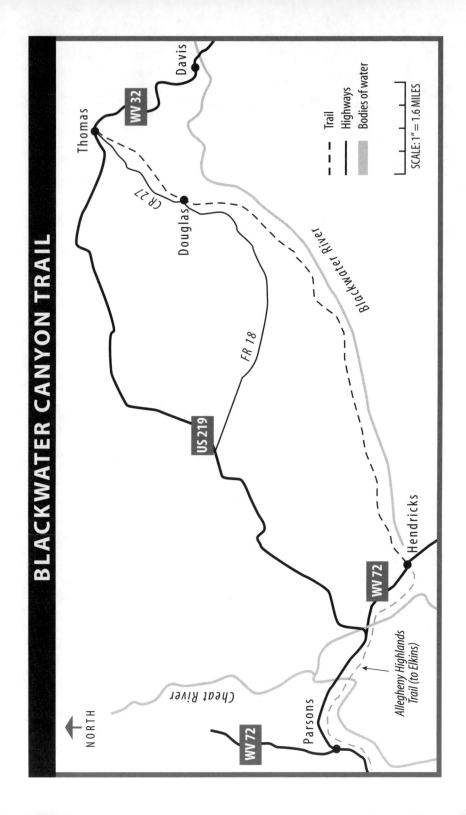

BLACKWATER CANYON TRAIL

NORTH

Davis

WV 32

Thomas

CR 27

Douglas

Blackwater River

FR 18

US 219

Hendricks

WV 72

Cheat River

Parsons

WV 72

Allegheny Highlands
Trail (to Elkins)

Trail
Highways
Bodies of water

SCALE: 1" = 1.6 MILES

Thomas to Hendricks and took advantage of about 1,200 feet of elevation loss. The elevation at Thomas is around 3,040 feet, while Hendricks is just at around 1,800 feet, so make it easy on yourself and start in Thomas.

Due to the lack of maintenance, the Forest Service suggests that people walk or ride in front of their kids in order to warn them of danger and to always stay on the uphill side of the grade so that you are not trespassing on private property. We rode with our two young kids, one on a trailer bike and one on a kid's bike, with very little trouble.

Just outside of Thomas, you will ride past coke ovens that line the mountainside, reminiscent of the days when the railroad was used to haul timber and coal out of the canyon. This ride became one of the

most memorable rides of my life, and is forever sketched in my memory as a photograph from this ride appeared on the cover of a November 2005 *Wonderful West Virginia Magazine*. The photograph shows me with the kids standing on a large rock, looking up at a spectacular 20-foot waterfall spilling into a pristine pool of water. We were told by locals to listen for the waterfall, which isn't visible from the trail, but is just a short hike through the woods. We actually found a couple of smaller waterfalls before we came to this one—awesome in and of themselves. But, this waterfall was absolutely breathtaking. This is a ride to do at least once in your lifetime—and I hope it is around for people to enjoy for years to come.

Once in Hendricks, you can connect to the Allegheny Highlands Trail that starts here. This trail (page 99), will take you on to the town of Parsons, then on down all the way to Elkins. If you are wanting to do a two day out and back trip from Thomas, then riding on to Parsons from Hendricks would allow many more choices for lodging.

Length: 10.2 miles
Surface: Packed rock and soil, varied roughness
Allowed Uses: H, B, E

County: Tucker
Endpoints: Hendricks and Thomas
Access Points: Thomas F/W, Hendricks F/W
Note: Follows N. Fork Blackwater River, waterfalls, no maintenance. Also connects in Hendricks with the Allegheny Highlands Trail.
Contact: Julie Fosbender, Monongahela National Forest 304-257-4488 x14, jfosbender@fs.fed.us
Trail Roughness: ★★★
Scenery: ★★★★

Directions:

From Charleston to Thomas trailhead: Take I-79 North to Exit 99, US 119 North/US 33 East. Continue onto US 219 North. follow US 219 North to Thomas. At Thomas, take WV 32 South (Spruce Street). Turn right onto Douglas Rd, which crosses the trail. Turn left off Douglas Road onto the trail (you can drive on this portion) to reach the trailhead approximately a mile down the road. A Forest Service gate marks the trailhead, where there is space for parking.

From Charleston to Hendricks trailhead: Take I-79 North to Exit

99, US 119 North/US 33 East. Continue onto US 219 North. follow US 219 North to Parsons. Turn right onto WV 72 to Hendricks. Turn right on Second Street. The trailhead is on the right. Look for the gazebo and parking at the trailhead.

WHERE TO STAY AND DINE:

The Purple Fiddle & Fiddlers Roost
Bed & Breakfast, Dining
Thomas, WV 26292
304-463-4040

Black Bear Resort
Cortland Road
Davis, WV 26260
304-866-4391

Canaan Valley Resort & State Park
Rt. 32 North
Davis, WV 26260
1-800-CALL-WVA

Blue Ridge Restaurant
Rt. 32
Thomas, WV 20292
304-463-4291

Shuttle Service:
Highland Scene Tours
Rt. 32
Davis, WV 26260
304-259-5889

19. ALLEGHENY HIGHLANDS TRAIL

This almost 25-mile trail meanders through one of the most beautiful areas of the state, from Elkins to Hendricks (though it can be ridden just as easily from Hendricks to Elkins). The trail is always close to US 219, and crosses it twice. Allegheny Highlands Trail begins in the charming town of Elkins, where you'll want to check out the Elkins Depot (the future southern AHT trailhead) and home of the Elkins Welcome Center. The trail follows the route of the old West Virginia Central and Pittsburgh railway built in 1884 by Henry Gassaway Davis.

If you want to begin your ride/hike with a good meal, be sure to try the crab cake or fish sandwiches at Fresh Bay Seafood, near the trailhead at Highland Park; the Visitors Center is also located here. The first four miles of the trail are paved, making it ideal for road bikes, inline skates or strollers. The trail eventually turns to rolled limestone sand.

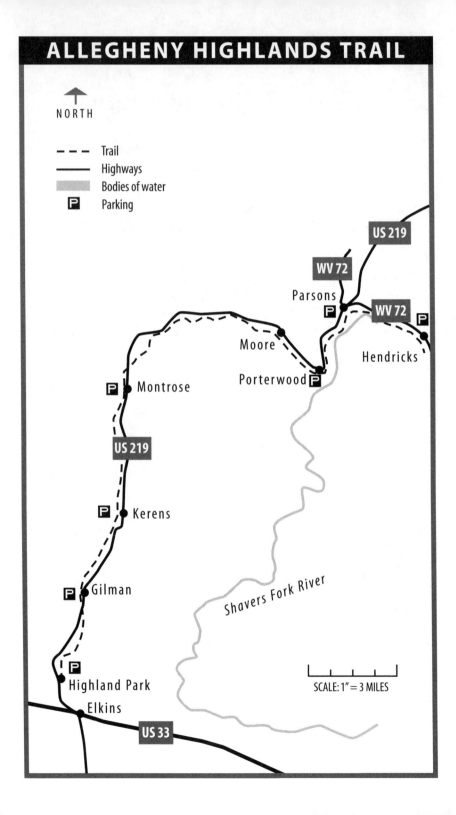

ALLEGHENY HIGHLANDS TRAIL

NORTH

- - - Trail
— Highways
▨ Bodies of water
🅿 Parking

US 219

WV 72

Parsons
🅿

WV 72 🅿

Moore

Hendricks

Porterwood 🅿

🅿 Montrose

US 219

🅿 Kerens

Shavers Fork River

🅿 Gilman

🅿 Highland Park

Elkins

SCALE: 1" = 3 MILES

US 33

The rolled limestone sand is between paved sections on either end. The pavement starts again at Porterwood and goes all the way to Hendricks. The paved section on both ends is almost 12 miles, the unpaved middle is about 13 miles.

You will ride through quaint farms and majestic forest. Unlike most trails, which are fairly flat, this trail gently rolls up and down through the mountains. Along the rail trail you will find at least 11 adjacent trails and several country roads, allowing you to extend your ride if you like.

The well-marked trail passes through the communities of Gilman, Kerens, Montrose and Porterwood. Between Kerens and Montrose you will ride through a wetlands area, a favorite spot for bird watchers looking for waterfowl.

Montrose, about 10 miles from Highland Park, is a good place for a rest with a shelter for riders. We enjoyed a stop at a flea market with a sign out front reading "Fantastically Large Yard Sale," known locally as the FLY market. We treated ourselves to some ice cream here.

Parsons is the largest town on the trail besides Elkins. Even though it is near the end of the trail, this is the best place for a lunch or rest break. The city has taken ownership of the railroad bridge and plans to rehab the bridge for future trail use.

The AHT borders the Monongahela National Forest in Tucker County, where you can access single-track trails, including South Haddix and Shingle Tree, on Pheasant Mountain. We also stopped in at the town's country grocery store, where we sat with some locals who were playing guitar and singing folk songs. Unfortunately we have heard this place is no longer in business. We used the Highland Scenic Tours Shuttle Service, which was very reliable and reasonably priced.

This trail and the Blackwater Canyon Trail (page 93) both end in Hendricks, making it easy to link the two trails for a much longer ride. Adventuresome riders will want to ride all the way from Thomas to Elkins, or vice versa, for a ride of over 35 miles.

Distance: 24.6 miles
Surface: 13 miles packed sand, 11.6 miles asphalt
Allowed Uses: H, B, E, S, X, A
Counties: Randolph, Tucker
Endpoints: Elkins and Hendricks
Access Points: Elkins F/W, Parsons F/W, Hendricks F/W, Gilman, Kerens, Montrose, Porterwood

Note: Links to Blackwater Canyon Rail Trail

Contact: Highlands Trail Foundation, Karen@elkinsbike.com, www. highlandstrail.org

Trail Roughness: ★★★

Scenery: ★★★★

Directions:

From Charleston to Elkins: Take I-79 North to Exit 99. Get on US 119 North/US 33 East and follow to WV 92. take a slight right onto WV 92 South into Elkins. Turn left on US 219 North to access the southernmost trailhead, Highland Park, located across from the Division of Highways District 8 Headquarters a mile from downtown Elkins. Note that the mileage is marked with the Elkins depot as 0, so milepost 1 is only about .2 mile from the Highland Park trailhead.

The Gilman, Kerens, Montrose, and Porterwood trailheads are located mid-trail off US 219, also. Each has parking facilities.

To Parsons: Continue on US 219 North to Parsons. Parking available in town anywhere on Main Street, 1st Street, or side streets.

To Hendricks: Continue following US 219 North to the northern trailhead located at the intersection of Main and 3rd Streets in Hendricks.

WHERE TO STAY AND DINE:

The Purple Fiddle & Fiddlers Roost
Bed & Breakfast, Dining
Thomas, WV 26292
304-463-4040

Holiday Inn Express
50 Martin Street
Elkins, WV 26241
1- 877- 508- 1762

Elkins Motor Lodge
830 Harrison Avenue
Elkins, WV 26241

Sirianni's Café
Davis, WV 26260
304-259-5454

Canaan Valley Resort & State Park
Rt. 32 North
Davis, WV 26260
1-800-CALL-WVA

Shuttle Service:
Highland Scene Tours
Rt. 32
Davis, WV 26260
304-259-5889

OTHER:

Joey's Bike Shop
101 Johnson Avenue
Elkins, WV 26241
304-636-0219

Blackwater Bikes
Rt. 32
Davis, WV 26260
304-259-5286

Blackwater Falls State Park
Rt. 32
Davis, WV
304-259-5216

20. WEST FORK RAIL TRAIL

The West Fork Rail Trail feels more like a railroad than any other rail trail in the state. It follows the old Coal & Iron Railroad that ran from Elkins to Durbin, which started in 1903 and was sold to the Western Maryland Railway in 1905. The railway was used originally to haul vast amounts of timber from the Cheat Mountain area. In 1986, the long abandoned line was converted to a rail trail.

The trail starts in Durbin and goes to Glady. The soothing rumble of the river complements the trail's serene environment. This is a great path for biking, but the surface is primarily ballast left over from the rail corridor, so leave your road bike at home.

Durbin is an old-fashioned railroad town, where you still hear the whistle of the Rocket train as it chugs through town. Home of the Durbin Depot, this is the trail to ride/hike if you are looking not only for scenery and exercise, but also for a good history lesson about the state's rich railroad heritage.

We stayed at the Greenbrier Suites, owned by Frank Proud, one of

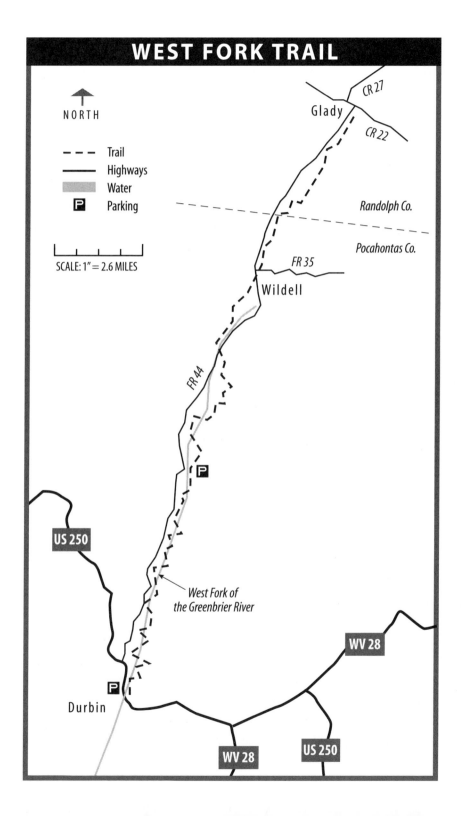

WEST FORK TRAIL

NORTH

- - - - Trail
——— Highways
▨▨▨ Water
P Parking

SCALE: 1" = 2.6 MILES

Glady

CR 27

CR 22

Randolph Co.

Pocahontas Co.

FR 35

Wildell

FR 44

P

US 250

West Fork of
the Greenbrier River

WV 28

P

Durbin

WV 28

US 250

the most active WVRTC members. His place in downtown Durbin is cozy, super convenient and has a balcony overlooking Durbin's Main Street and the train depot. (He recently expanded, adding private cottages.)

We started our ride by taking a private shuttle to Glady, where we found a well-marked trailhead and immediately began riding through farm country.

The pleasant 23-mile trail snakes its way through a remote mountain setting and follows the West Fork of the Greenbrier River for most of its route, crosses the Pocahontas/Randolph County line and enters the watershed of the Cheat, picking up the West Fork of the Glady River here. The county line is at an elevation of 3,147 feet. The trail follows an old forest road, FR 44, the entire way. The trail is accessible in several points from FR 44 along the way.

For the first five miles, the trail takes a higher route above the western side of the West Fork River and winds in and out of wooded areas, offering great views of the surrounding mountains. At about seven miles in, you'll cross a long wooden bridge, a place we chose to stop and eat lunch. The trail soon levels out with the river for the remaining 17 miles to the town of Durbin following the Glady Fork River southward. As

you make your way through the mountains, the trail and the river make sweeping sharp turns through the valley surrounded by steep hillsides. For most of the trail, other than the gravel forest road (FR 44), there are few signs of civilization other than the trail itself.

The West Fork River is a popular fishing spot; we saw several anglers along the way. In summer, be sure to bring your swimsuit, there are several deep pools and places to take a relaxing break and cool off.

The trail comes to an end in Durbin. Bike shuttles are available through Greenbrier Suites and Highland Scenic Tours for one way rides.

Milepost:

299.2 Glady
302.0 Beulah
302.7 Summit Cut
305.8 Wildell
313.9 Burner
316.1 Braucher
319.6 Olive
321.8 Durbin

Length: 22.6 miles
Surface: Packed stone
Allowed Uses: H, B, E, X
Counties: Pocahontas, Randolph
Endpoints: Glady and Durbin
Note: Follows W. Fork of the Greenbrier River & W. Fork of Glady
  Fork River
Contact: Pocahontas County CVB 1-800-336-7009
Trail Roughness: ★★★
Scenery: ★★★

Directions:
  From Charleston to Glady trailhead: Take I-79 North to Exit 99.
Get on US 119 north/US 33 East to WV 92. Take a right onto WV 92
South/US 33 East. Follow US 33 East to CR 27. Turn right onto CR
27 (Glady Road) and take this road about 10 miles to Glady. When you
come to the intersection of Glady and Elliots Roads, continue straight

on Glady through the stop sign and follow the road for approximately a quarter mile to where it dead-ends. The trailhead will be directly in front of you.

From Charleston to Durbin trailhead: Take I-79 North to Exit 99. Get on US 119 North/US 33 East to WV 92. Take a right onto WV 92 South. Follow WV 92 South/US 250 South to Durbin. Look for the trailhead on the left about a mile before you reach the town.

WHERE TO STAY AND DINE:

Greenbrier Suites (& Shuttle Service)
Main Street
Durbin, WV 26264
1-800-510-0180

The Purple Fiddle & Fiddlers Roost
Bed & Breakfast, Dining
Thomas, WV 26292
304-463-4040

Holiday Inn Express
50 Martin Street
Elkins, WV 26241
1- 877- 508- 1762

Elkins Motor Lodge
830 Harrison Avenue
Elkins, WV 26241

Sirianni's Café
Rt. 32
Davis, WV 26260
304-259-5454

Canaan Valley Resort & State Park
Rt. 32 North
Davis, WV 26260
304-866-4121

Highland Scenic Tours Shuttle Service
Rt. 32
Davis, WV 26260
304-259-5889

OTHER:

The Durbin Depot
Main Street
Durbin, WV 26264
877-686-7245

Blackwater Bikes
Rt. 32
Davis, WV 26260
304-259-5286

Blackwater Falls State Park
Rt. 32
Davis, WV
304-259-5216

21. GREENBRIER RIVER TRAIL

A former C & O Railway, this magnificent 77-mile trail is arguably one of the best rail trails in the country. As you wind your way through the scenic Greenbrier River Valley, you'll see Monongahela National Forest, Cass Scenic Railroad State Park, Seneca State Forest, Watoga State Park, Calvin Price State Forest, and Greenbrier State Forest. You'll be treated to 25 bridges and two tunnels, all the while surrounded by the beauty of the Allegheny Mountains.

This trail gets its name from the Greenbrier River—called *Ronce Verte* by French explorers, most likely a reference to the green briers that grow along the river. Its conversion from a railway to a rail trail is most often credited to the efforts of Mark Ligon Hankins, who convinced CSX to give the trail to the state. The trail can easily be ridden in sections or in its totality as an epic one-to-three-day adventure. We chose to ride the trail in several portions—making for multiple fun trips, some with kids and some without. Though the mile markers actually start at the southern trailhead, we rode the rail trail at the northern trailhead at Cass

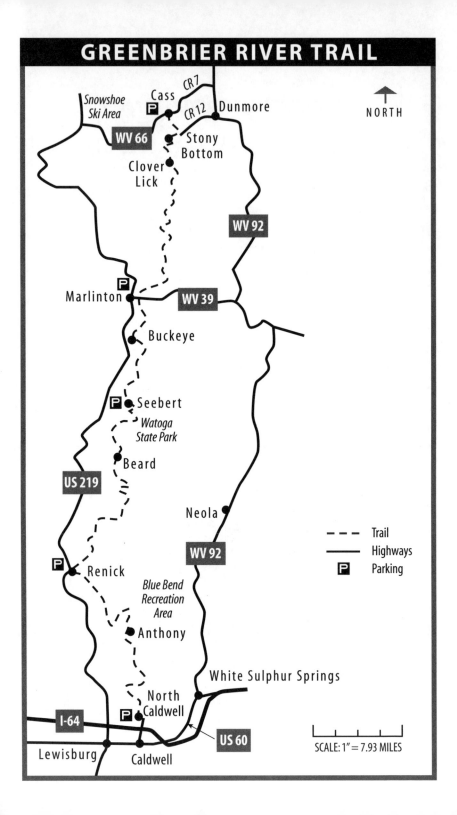

GREENBRIER RIVER TRAIL

NORTH

Snowshoe Ski Area

CR 7

Cass

P

CR 12

Dunmore

WV 66

Stony Bottom

Clover Lick

WV 92

P Marlinton

WV 39

Buckeye

P Seebert

Watoga State Park

Beard

US 219

Neola

WV 92

P Renick

Blue Bend Recreation Area

Anthony

White Sulphur Springs

North Caldwell

I-64

P

US 60

Lewisburg

Caldwell

– – – Trail
——— Highways
P Parking

SCALE: 1" = 7.93 MILES

Scenic Railroad State Park and followed the river downstream for a slight downhill ride.

The Cass trailhead is located about one mile from the large parking lot at the Cass General Store and Cass Scenic RR depot. Unfortunately, there are no signs from the Cass parking lot to the trailhead. To reach the trailhead from the Cass parking lot, see directions further in this chapter.

The first town you will pass is the charming little town of Clover Lick, where you'll see an old-time railroad depot. We really enjoyed the next 20 or so miles of trail, which was "wild & wonderful" West Virginia at its finest—lush green valleys surrounded by mountains, white-capped river water breaking on giant rocks and amazing wildflower

meadows. At mile marker 65, you'll pass through the first tunnel, Sharps Tunnel. It was named for the Sharp family, who owned the land and gave access to the railways. Also, keep an eye out for a restored train water tower just north of Marlinton.

The trail continues into Marlinton at mile marker 55, the county seat of Pocahontas and the largest town (pop. 1,200) on the trail. Unfortunately the town's restored yellow train station, which used to sit along the trail and offer visitors information,

was destroyed by fire. You can now get information at the Visitors Center on 2nd Avenue.

The five-mile trail section near Marlinton holds special sentimental value to me, as it is part of the Great Greenbrier River Race, which I do with my son the last Saturday each April. After running three miles through Marlinton and kayaking four miles down the Greenbrier River, we ride five miles down to the old town of Watoga and five miles back on the rail trail. Even while racing, it is hard not to pay attention to the surrounding beauty.

Marlinton, considered a hip and laid-back mountain town, has some great places to eat and stay (and makes a nice place for an overnight for those who are riding the whole trail). You will definitely want to make time to visit the Dirtbean, a very cool café, coffee house, bike shop and fitness/coaching facility, located on 8th Street in downtown Marlinton.

We stayed at Locust Hill Bed & Breakfast, which also has a day spa. The grounds surrounding Locust Hill are gorgeous; we enjoyed sitting on a bench at the inn looking out at the pond. After leaving Marlinton, you'll head to Seebert, which is the home of Watoga State Park. Along the way you'll cross an interesting rustic steel bridge. Next, you'll head to the town of Beard, which is approximately the trail's halfway point.

A short ways past Beard, look for the concrete posts with engraved "W's; these are reminders for the train engineer to blow the whistle at an upcoming crossing. At about mile marker 31, you'll come to the 402-foot-long Droop Mountain Tunnel, built in 1900 and cut directly into solid rock; jagged rock walls surround you as you cross through the mountain. As you continue on your way past Anthony at mile marker 15, the trail goes by some pretty wide and scenic spots on the river—to the southern terminus at Caldwell, near the world famous Greenbrier

Hotel. This trailhead is just outside Lewisburg, where you can find dining, lodging and shopping. We highly recommend West Virginia Tourism's Greenbrier River Rail Trail map and Jim Hudson's excellent book *Rail Trails Along the Greenbrier River*. The Greenbrier River Trail Association has erected interpretive signs along the trail, and they are worth stopping at for their take on local history and tips on what to look for along the trail.

If you choose to start your ride from the Lewisburg end, you can access the trail from US 60 traveling east from Lewisburg, turning left after about 1/2 mile onto Stonehouse Road. You continue about one mile before reaching the trail's parking lot on your left. Note that the trail begins at mile marker 3. (The "first" three miles originally planned for this trail have never been completed.) This end of the trail is incredibly scenic. Along the trail you'll find many swimming areas with lots of big rocks, picnic areas and nice benches. One of the first things you will

see is Camp Allegheny, a camp for girls that has been in operation for more than 50 years.

Note at mile marker 5 there are steps allowing you to walk down to the river. Local Boy Scouts built these steps. At about mile 13 you'll find a beautiful boat landing, perfect for launching canoes or kayaks or for wading. Start your ride with a visit to Free Spirit Adventures, just three miles from the trailhead on US 60 east between Caldwell and White Sulphur Springs. The bike shop offers shuttles anywhere along the Greenbrier River Trail as well as bike rentals, tours, service and repairs, and even a cycling school.

If you have time be sure to check out Lewisburg, set in the beautiful Greenbrier River Valley and the site of an 1862 Civil War battle. For an extra treat on your ride, stay at the General Lewis Inn, where you can enjoy the scenery from rocking chairs on a long shaded veranda. If you're feeling really brave, ask to stay in one of their "haunted" rooms. Lewisburg is the largest town along the rail trail and is a mecca of shopping, fine restaurants and quaint bed & breakfasts. Locals say Lewisburg is the "Boulder" of the East Coast, with an eclectic blend of coffee houses, art galleries, pottery shops and some of the best dining in the state.

Mileage:

Mile 3: North Caldwell - Southern Terminus - 1.3 miles north of US 60 at Caldwell on CR 38 (Stonehouse Road).
• Parking area, information, drinking water and picnic tables.
• Groceries, post office and public phone nearby in Caldwell - 1.5 miles.

- Fee camping at nearby at Greenbrier State Forest, 2 miles east on US 60, follow signs.
- Canoe access nearby (across US 60 - Caldwell Boat Launch).

Mile 4.7:
- Trailside campsite, table and fire ring, toilet.

Mile 5.8: Harper (Hopper) - from CR 38, take CR 38/2 to CR 30/3.
- Trail access point, limited parking.

Mile 11.1: Keister - from CR 38, take CR 30 to CR 30/1.
- Trail access point, limited parking.

Mile 13.5:
- Trailside campsite, table and fire ring, toilet, and drinking water.

Mile 14: Anthony - from US 219, at Frankford, 4.9 miles on CR 21and CR 21/2.
- Trail access point, parking, canoe access.
- Groceries, supplies, post office, fee camping at Blue Bend and public phone nearby.

Mile 20.5: Toilet

Mile 21.5: Spring Creek - from US 219, 1.5 miles north of Frankford, east 3.5 miles on CR 13.
- Trail access, limited parking, canoe access.

Mile 24.5: Renick - from US 219, east 0.4 miles on CR 11 (Auto Road).
- Trail access, parking, canoe access.
- Groceries, post office and public phone along US 219.

Mile 28.5:
- Trailside campsite, table and fire ring, toilet, and drinking water.

Mile 29.6: Horrock - from US 219 at Renick, east 4.1 miles on CR 7 (Brownstown Road), then 1.2 miles on CR 7/1 to CR 7/2 (Rorer Road), 0.5 miles to trail.
• Trail access point, limited parking.

Mile 30.9: Droop Mountain Tunnel - 402 feet.

Mile 33.7:
• Trailside camping, table and fire ring, toilet.

Mile 38.5: Beard - from US 219 at Hillsboro, follow CR 31 (Denmar Road), 6 miles to CR 31/8 (Beard P.O. Road), 0.3 miles to trail.
• Trail access point, parking, and horse trailer parking.
• Canoe access.
• Lodging nearby (Bed and Breakfast).

Mile 40.9: Trailside campsite
• Table and fire ring.

Mile 41.7: Burnsides - from US 219 at Hillsboro, follow CR 31 (Denmar Road), 1.3 miles to CR 31/1 (Workman Road), 1 mile to trail.
• Trail access point, limited parking, canoe access.

Mile 45.8: Seebert - from US 219 north of Hillsboro, follow CR 27 (Seebert Road), 2 miles to trail.
• Trail access point, parking, and horse trailer parking.
• Canoe access point.
• Fee camping available at Watoga State Park, across bridge, 2 miles.
• Cabins (by reservation), meals, drinking water, and public phone available at Watoga State Park.
• Groceries, supplies and public phone available in Seebert.

Mile 46: Seebert - from Seebert Road follow CR 27 (River Road) 1 mile. (See above), trail access, limited parking.

Mile 47: Steven Hole Run - follow CR 27 (River Road) 1 mile.
• Trail access point, limited parking.

Mile 47.9: Watoga Bridge - Trail crosses to east side of Greenbrier River on old truss type railroad bridge. The two sections of this bridge were constructed at different times due to a spectacular train wreck here on May 4, 1924. The North span is part of the original bridge constructed in 1899/1900, while the southern span was constructed in 1925, to replace the span lost the year before.

Mile 48.1: Site of old town of Watoga, a logging boom town in the early 1900s. Remains of old bank safe may be seen east side of trail. Watoga was the site of a large sawmill and a kindling wood factory in the early 1900s.

Mile 49.3: Mouth of Beaver Creek trailside campsite. Also site of old town of Violet (later called Dan). A logging railroad which ran up Beaver Creek also followed the mainline tracks south to the lumber mill at the town of Watoga.
• Table and fire ring, toilet.

Mile 51.4:
• Trailside campsite, table and fire ring.

Mile 52.2: Buckeye - from US 219 at Buckeye, follow CR 219/15, 1mile to trail.
• Trail access point, limited parking.

Mile 55.1: Stillwell Park (Marlinton Municipal Park) - from WV 39 in Marlinton, follow CR 39/2, 1.5 miles to park.
• Trail access point, parking and horse trailer parking.
• Camping, toilets and water available, canoe access.

Mile 55.8: Knapps Creek Bridge - this 2nd bridge was constructed in 1929 to replace the original which was completed in 1900.

Mile 56: Marlinton - 9th Street crossing (behind the elementary school).
• Trail access point, parking.
• Groceries, lodging, meals, post office, drinking water and hospital nearby.

Mile 56.1: Marlinton Depot - depot was constructed in 1901
• Trail access point, parking.
• Information and accessible restrooms.
• A two mile section is paved for wheelchair access between MP 56.1 and MP 54.1. Mile Post 56.5: Water tank - only remaining water tank on GRT, built in 1923 and currently under restoration. The remains of the C&O turntable may be found on the downstream side of the water tank, 50 feet from the trail.

Mile 62.4: Clawson - follow CR 11/2 from WV 28 at Dilly's Mill, 5 miles over the mountain to trail. Extremely difficult route, not recommended for the faint of heart!
• Trail access point, very limited parking.

Mile 63.7:
• Trailside campsite (NO horses please)
• Table, fire ring and camping shelter, toilet, and drinking water.

Mile 65.7: Sharp's Tunnel and bridge—built in 1900, tunnel is 511 feet long and bridge is 229 feet long.

Mile 67.1: Big Run - trailside picnic shelter adjacent to small waterfall and pool in Big Run.

Mile 69.6:
• Trailside campsite (one equestrian site)
• Table and fire ring, toilet and drinking water.

Mile 71.1: Clover Lick - from WV 28 north of Seneca State Forest,

take CR 1/4 (Laurel Run Road), 4.2 miles to Clover Lick.
• Trail access, parking.
• Canoe access.
• Recently renovated, the C&O depot was built near the turn of the century, and originally stood south of the road crossing.
• Old bridge piers in river provided rail service to the Raine Lumber Company band mill on the east side of the river from 1913 to 1929.

Mile 71.1: Clover Lick

Mile 74.5: Stony Bottom - from WV 66, 1 mile west of Cass, take CR 1 (Back Mountain Road), south 3.1 miles.
• Trail access point, lodging, and public phone.

Mile 77: Sitlington - from WV 28 south of Dunmore, take CR 12 (Sitlington Road), 4 miles.
• Trail access point, limited parking, canoe access.

Mile 78.5: Raywood - site of former sawmill town. The piers in the river supported a bridge and tracks to the Warn Lumber Company Mill, which operated from 1914 to 1928.

Mile 79.4: Deer Creek - follow CR 1/13 (Deer Creek Road), 1 mile to trail.
• Trail access point, limited parking.

Mile 80.4: Cass - Northern Terminus - follow CR 1/13 (Deer Creek Road), .1 miles to parking area.
• Trail access and parking area.
• Canoe access.
• Lodging, camping, public phone, food service, post office, gift shops, first aid, drinking water and groceries nearby.
• Cabins (by reservation) and train rides available at Cass Scenic Railroad StatePark.

Length: 77 miles

Surface: Packed gravel, 5 miles asphalt Marlinton-Buckeye

Allowed Uses: H, B

County: Pocahontas, Greenbrier

Endpoints: Cass and Caldwell

Access Points: North Caldwell F/W, Marlinton F/W, Clover Lick, Cass, F/W, Seebert F/W (Recommended by the Greenbrier River Trail Assoc.)

Note: 2 tunnels, physically challenged access in Marlinton

Contact: Pocahontas County CVB 1-800-336-7009,
         www.GreenbrierRiverTrail.com

Trail Roughness: ★★

Scenery: ★★★

Directions are listed by trailhead:

North Caldwell

    From Charleston, WV: Take I-64 East to Exit 175, White Sulphur Springs. Turn left on US 60 West and go about 2 miles to the Greenbrier River bridge. Cross bridge and immediately turn right onto Stonehouse Road. Go 1 mile to the trailhead. Parking is on the left, the trail is on the right.

    From Morgantown, WV: Take I-79 South to Exit 57, then US 19 South. Left on WV 39 East, then right on WV 20 South. Then left on US 60 east. Go to the Greenbrier River and just before crossing the bridge, turn left onto Stonehouse Road. Go 1 mile to the trailhead. Parking is on the left, the trail is on the right.

    From Richmond, VA: Take I-64 West to Exit 175, White Sulphur Springs. Turn right on ramp and then left on US 60 West and go about 2 miles to the Greenbrier River bridge. Cross bridge and immediately turn right onto Stonehouse Road. Go 1 mile to the trailhead. Parking is on the left, the trail is on the right.

Seebert

    From Charleston, WV: Take I-64 East to Exit 169 in Lewisburg.

Left on US 219 North. Follow US 219 North thru Hillsboro to CR 27/Seebert Road. Turn right on Seebert Road toward Watoga State Park. Go about a mile to Seebert. The trail crosses the road immediately before the bridge across the Greenbrier River. At the trail crossing, left on the trail is north toward Marlinton, and right on the trail is south toward North Caldwell.

From Morgantown, WV: Take I-79 South to Exit 57, then US 19 South. Left on WV 55 East which eventually becomes WV 55/WV 39/Marlinton Road. Then right on US 219 South, then left on CR 27/Seebert Road toward Watoga State Park. Go about a mile to Seebert. The trail crosses the road immediately before the bridge across the Greenbrier River. At the trail crossing, left on the trail is north toward Marlinton, and right on the trail is south toward North Caldwell.

From Richmond, VA: Take I-64 West to Exit 220 on VA 262 toward US 11. Merge onto VA 262 North, then take the VA 254/Parkersburg Turnpike. Continue onto VA 42 South, then VA 39. Then left onto US 220 South, then take the 2nd right onto VA 39 West. Enter West Virginia. Left on US 219 South/WV 39 West. Then left at the sign for Watoga State Park at CR 27/Seebert Road. Go about a mile to Seebert. The trail crosses the road immediately before the bridge across the Greenbrier River. At the trail crossing, left on the trail is north toward Marlinton, and right on the trail is south toward North Caldwell.

Marlinton

From Charleston, WV: Take I-64 East to Exit 175 in White Sulphur Springs. Go thru town and get on WV 92 North, which you take to the junction at WV 92 and WV 39. Go left onto WV 39 West into Marlinton. The trail crosses WV 39 at the old railroad depot. Trailhead parking is available at the depot.

From Morgantown, WV: Take I-79 South to Exit 57, then US 19 South. Left on WV 55 East which eventually becomes WV 55/WV 39/Marlinton Road. The trail crosses WV 39 at the old railroad depot. Trailhead parking is available at the depot.

From Richmond, VA: Take I-64 West to Exit 220 on VA 262 toward US 11. Merge onto VA 262 North, then take the VA 254/Parkersburg Turnpike. Continue onto VA 42 South, then VA 39. Then left onto US 220 South, then take the 2nd right onto VA 39 West. Enter West Virginia. Continue onto WV 39 West into Marlinton. The trail crosses WV 39 at the old railroad depot. Trailhead parking is available at the depot.

Cass

Finding the trail! The Cass trailhead of the Greenbrier River Trail is located about one mile from the large parking lot at the Cass General Store and Cass Scenic railroad depot. Unfortunately, there are no signs from the Cass parking lot to the trailhead. To reach the trailhead from the Cass parking lot cross the railroad tracks and follow the road as it turns right, uphill past the General Store and the post office. Immediately turn left on Back Mountain Road toward Stoney Bottom. Follow through the town of Cass for about 3/8 mile to Deer Creek Road at the edge of town. Turn left onto gravel-covered Deer Creek Road (at the only sign "To Greenbrier River Trail") and go about 1/2 mile, past the last house and the stacks of old railroad ties. The old railroad right of way is on the left and the trailhead parking is straight ahead. From the trailhead parking lot, the trail goes south (downstream) toward Marlinton.

PARKING CAUTION *The Greenbrier River Trail trailhead at Cass is located in an isolated area and is not visible from any nearby roads or houses.* Although the crime rate in rural WV is the lowest in the country,

this trailhead is not a good spot to leave your car, especially overnight. Instead, consider parking at the large parking lot in Cass and riding your bicycle one mile to the trailhead. Beware, the road through town has a couple of short, steep hills, and does have some car traffic.

From Charleston, WV: Take I-64 East to Exit 175 in White Sulphur Springs. Go thru town and get on WV 92 North, which you take to the junction at WV 92 and WV 39. Go left onto WV 92/WV 39, then turn right onto WV 92 North at Minnehaha Springs. Take WV 92 North, then go left on WV 66 West/Cass Road. Follow Cass Road to Cass State Park and see directions for parking at the trailhead on the previous page.

From Morgantown, WV: Take the Kingwood Pike to WV 92 South at Reedsville. Go right and follow WV 92 South, eventually becoming WV 92 South/US 219 South/US 250 South. Stay on WV 92 South, then left onto WV 28 South, and shortly after, make a right on WV 66 West/Cass Road. Follow Cass Road to Cass State Park and see directions for parking at the trailhead on the previous page.

From Richmond, VA: Take I-64 West to Exit 220 on VA 262 toward US 11. Merge onto VA 262 North. Go left on US 250 West. Enter West Virginia. Go left at WV 92 South/WV 28 South. Then go right on WV 66 West/Cass Road. Follow Cass Road to Cass State Park and see directions for parking at the trailhead on the previous page.

WHERE TO STAY AND DINE:

In or near Cass:

Locust Hill Bed & Breakfast
1525 Locust Hill
Marlinton, WV 24954
1-800-617-0530

Snowshoe Mountain Resort & Restaurants
10 Snowshoe Drive
Snowshoe, WV 26209
304-572-1000

Elk River Touring Center Inn & Restaurant
US 219
Slatyfork, WV 26291
304-572-3771

Dirtbean Café Inn and Bike Shop
217 8th Street
Marlinton, WV 24954
304-799-4038

Hillsboro House B & B
Rt. 219
Hillsboro, WV 24946
304-653-4895

Greenbrier River Cabins
River Road
Seebert, WV 24946
304- 653-4646

Greenbrier River Lodge
Rt. 27
Seebert, WV 24946
800-982-5263

The Pretty Penny
Watoga State Park
Seebert, WV 24946
304-799-COIN

Appalachian Sport Lodge
3 Seneca Trail/Rt. 219
Marlinton, WV 24954
304-799-4050

Old Clark Inn
702 Third Avenue
Marlinton, WV 24954
800-849-4184

Jerico B&B and Pre-Civil War Cabins
Jerico Road
Marlinton, WV 24954
888-499-6241

Greenbrier Grill & Lodge
842 First Avenue
Marlinton, WV 24954
304-799-7233

EJ's Cottages and Horse Stabling
Sitlington Road
Dunmore, WV 24934
800-317-9120

Cass Scenic Railroad State Park
Rt. 66
Cass, WV 24927
1-800-call-wva

BICYCLE/KAYAK RENTALS:

Rt. 66 Outpost/Cass
304-456-4288

Appalachian Sport/Marlinton
304-799-4050

Dirtbean/Marlinton
304-799-4038

Jack Horner's Corner/Seebert
304-653-4515

OTHER:

Green Bank Observatory
Rt. 28/92
Green Bank, WV 24944
304-456-2011

In or near Lewisburg:

The General Lewis Inn & Restaurant
301 E. Washington Street
Lewisburg, WV 24901
304-645-2600

The Brier Inn
540 N. Jefferson Street
Lewisburg, WV 24901
304-645-7722

Fairfield Inn & Suites
273 Coleman Drive
Lewisburg, WV 24901
800-228-2800

Hampton Inn
30 Coleman Drive
Lewisburg, WV 24901
304-645-7300

Holiday Inn Express
222 Hunter Lane
Lewisburg, WV 24901
304-645-5750

The Old White Inn
865 E. Main Street
White Sulphur Springs, WV 24986
800-980-2441

Food & Friends
213 W. Washington Street
Lewisburg, WV 24901
304-645-4548

Irish Pub on Washington Street
109 E. Washington Street
Lewisburg, WV 24901
304-645-7386

The Market
215 W. Washington Street
Lewisburg, WV 24901
304-645-4084

Sam & Kitty's Kitchen
Rt. 60
Caldwell, WV 24925
304-647-4052

Stardust Café
102 E. Washington Street
Lewisburg, WV 24901
304-647-3663

Tavern 1785
208 W. Washington Street
Lewisburg, WV 24901
304-645-7744

OTHER:

Carnegie Hall WV
105 Church Street
Lewisburg, WV 24901
304-645-7917

22. GAULEY MOUNTAIN TRAIL

This trail can be ridden/hiked the same weekend—or even the same day—as the Williams River Trail. The Gauley Mountain trailhead is just a few miles away from the Williams River trailhead on the Scenic Highway. Coming from Richwood, the sign is clearly marked and on the left side of the highway.

Gauley Mountain Trail, while wider and less technical than Williams River Trail, still feels more like traditional trail riding/hiking than "rail trail" riding/hiking. There are several rock gardens and some twisted roots as well as multiple mud holes, some of which require some skill to maneuver around. The trail was fairly eroded when we were on it, but friends of the trail have received grant money to repair the trail in the near future. Though I've ridden this trail many times, one of my best memories is hiking this trail with my two kids and my mother. We had

a great time, enjoying nature as we chatted and made our way along the trail. We took time for a break and a picnic lunch in one of the prettier sections, surrounded by rhododendron.

For those who are well versed in single-track, there are multiple trails intersecting Gauley Mountain Trail that can be added to the route for a full day's riding/hiking. However, be forewarned that many of these trails are very advanced single-track trails. Though the trailhead is on the Scenic Highway, this trail

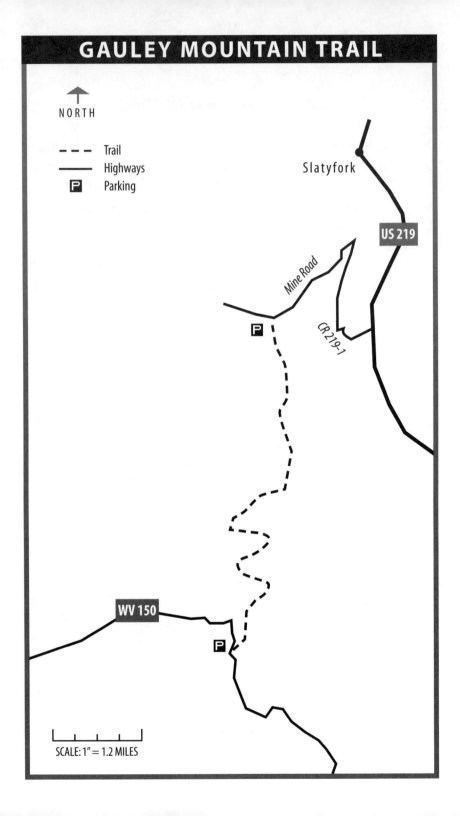

also can easily be accessed from the Elk River Touring Center, one of our favorite spots in West Virginia. The lodge has comfortable rooms, a restaurant with gourmet meals and a bike shop and guides, which can shuttle you to the trailhead or the trail ending point on Gauley Mountain's Mine Road.

For those wanting extra riding miles, Mine Road is just several miles from the lodge, followed by a 4-mile gradual gravel road climb to the trail entrance.

Length: 5.4 miles
Surface: Packed dirt and grass/rough single-track
Allowed uses: H, Mt. B, E, X
County: Pocahontas
Endpoints: WV 150 and Mine Road near Elk River Touring Center
Access Points: WV 150 (Scenic Highway), Mine Road (near Elk River Touring Center F/W)
Contact: Tim Henry, USFS 304-799-4334, www.fs.fed.us/r9/mnt
Trail Roughness: ★★★★
Scenery: ★★★

Directions:

From Marlinton, WV to Mine Road trailhead: Take US 219 North to just south of Slatyfork. Turn left on Mine Road/CR 219/1. Drive 3.5 miles on the gravel road to the trailhead on the left.

From Marlinton, WV to WV Scenic Highway trailhead: Take US 219 North to WV 150. Turn left on WV 150 and follow it 5 miles to the trailhead on the right.

WHERE TO STAY AND DINE:

Snowshoe Mountain Resort
10 Snowshoe Drive
Snowshoe, WV 26209
304-572-1000

Elk River Touring Center
US 219
Slatyfork, WV 26291
304-572-3771

Four Season's Lodge & Outdoor Center
Rt. 39
Richwood, WV 26261
800-829-4605

23. WILLIAMS RIVER TRAIL

Though only three miles long, this out-and-back rail trail is what wild, wonderful West Virginia is all about. Starting at Tea Creek Campground, just off of the Scenic Highway, this trail requires some single-track riding experience and a hardy bike or some advanced hiking skills. Coming from Richwood on WV 150, the Tea Creek Campground is clearly marked and is on the right side of the highway.

We actually rode the trail out and back with my 7-year-old, and while she had no problems, she was pretty exhausted afterward. My 11-year-old liked the trail so much he said we should build a house along the trail.

The trail is narrow in spots and has quite a few rocky and rooted sections as well as some gentle ups and downs. As you ride/hike along the bank of the Williams River you will feel more like you're on a roller coaster than a bike trail. We sat on giant boulders in the middle of a shallow part of the river and ate lunch, with whitewater rapids all around us. The end of the trail at Handley Public Hunting & Fishing Area is

not easily accessible by car, so you will have to turn around and hike or bike back out to the Tea Creek Campground, effectively making this a 6-mile trail out and back.

We spent the night at one of our favorite places, nearby Snowshoe Mountain Resort. Our room was conveniently located at the Inn at Snowshoe, which is at the bottom of the mountain, making for an easy half-hour drive to the Scenic Highway. The Inn boasts an indoor pool and game room, both big hits with the kids, as well as a family restaurant.

WILLIAMS RIVER TRAIL

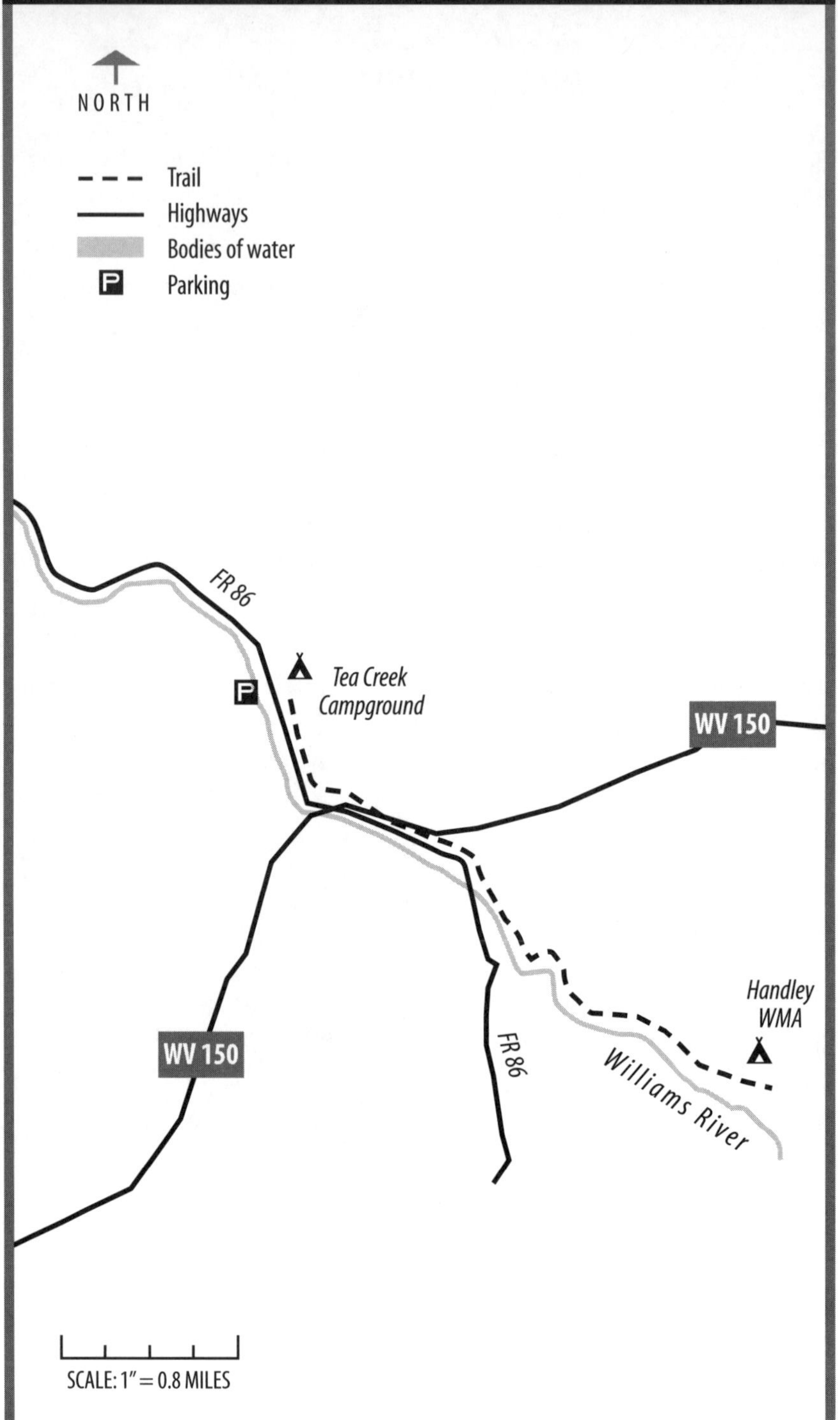

NORTH

- - - - Trail
——— Highways
▬▬▬ Bodies of water
🅿 Parking

FR 86

🅿

⛺ Tea Creek
Campground

WV 150

WV 150

FR 86

Handley
WMA
⛺

Williams River

SCALE: 1" = 0.8 MILES

During the spring and summer months Snowshoe Resort offers a shuttle to the top of the mountain, where you'll find mountain bike trails, a bike shop, restaurants, shopping and more lodging.

Length: 3 miles
Surface: Packed dirt and grass/rough single-track
Allowed uses: H, Mt. B, E, X
County: Pocahontas
Endpoints: Tea Creek Campground and Handley Public Hunting & Fishing Area
Access Points: WV 150 & FS Road 86 at Tea Creek Campground
Note: Hikers & equestrians can continue through Handley Public Fishing & Hunting Area. Bikes are not permitted in the Handley area.

Contact: Tim Henry, USFS 304-799-4334
Trail Roughness: ★★★★
Scenery: ★★★★

Directions:

From Marlinton take US 219 north 7 miles to WV 150, the Highland Scenic Highway. Turn left onto WV 150 and drive approximately 9 miles to the Williams River Bridge turnoff, located on the left. Turn left at the stop sign onto Forest Road 86 and drive 1 mile. The campground and trailhead are located on the right. The trailhead leaves from the parking area over the cement bridge.

WHERE TO STAY AND DINE:

Snowshoe Mountain Resort (Many excellent restaurants)
10 Snowshoe Drive
Snowshoe, WV 26209
304-572-1000

Elk River Touring Center (restaurant)
US 219
Slatyfork, WV 26291
304-572-3771

Four Season's Lodge & Outdoor Center
Rt. 39
Richwood, WV 26261
800-829-4605

24. CRANBERRY TRI-RIVERS RAIL TRAIL

Starting in Richwood, we rode this trail with the mayor, a city councilman, several friends of theirs and a dog. We stayed at the Four Seasons Inn, which was just up the road from the trailhead. Bruce Donaldson, an instrumental force in the construction and maintenance of the rail trail, owns the inn as well as Four Seasons Outfitters, which provides bike sales, rentals and service.

This trail is spectacular enough that it warrants a weekend-getaway trip to Richwood; you'll enjoy the small-town charm of the town, the friendliness of the townsfolk and the sights you'll see along the rail trail. Getting out on the trail is very easy, as the trailhead is in downtown Richwood, almost directly behind a historic train depot. The trail, though rough in spots, is a joy to ride and takes you on a scenic tour of three of West Virginia's most beautiful rivers—the Cranberry, the Cherry and the Gauley—following the Cherry and Gauley rivers and crossing the Cranberry. While there are a few other access points, we suggest you use Richwood as your base and do an out and back on this trail.

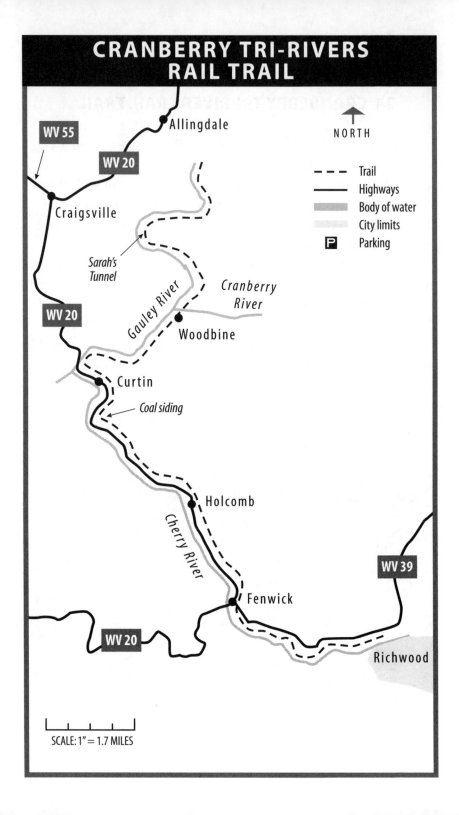

CRANBERRY TRI-RIVERS
RAIL TRAIL

WV 55

Allingdale

WV 20

NORTH

- - - Trail
——— Highways
Body of water
City limits
P Parking

Craigsville

Sarah's
Tunnel

Gauley River

Cranberry
River

WV 20

Woodbine

Curtin

Coal siding

Holcomb

Cherry River

WV 39

Fenwick

WV 20

Richwood

SCALE: 1" = 1.7 MILES

The first six miles of this trail pass numerous homes, where Mayor Bob Henry Baber seemed to know almost everyone.

Soon out of Richwood, the trail begins to parallel the Cherry River. Shortly after the trail crosses Rt. 55 in Holcomb, it enters Monongahela National Forest. Here, the trail becomes more remote. Keep your eyes open for a beautiful waterfall on the right. After you cross the Cranberry River, the trail takes you through the curving, 640-foot Sarah's Tunnel, which is pitch dark at its center. If you forgot to bring a light, take a deep breath and go for it. You'll be glad you did. One mile beyond the tunnel, you arrive at the trail's end. However, there are plans to extend the trail another 10 miles into the forest. The middle section of this trail between Holcomb and the Cranberry River is just amazing. This section has a somewhat smoother trail surface than the ends of the trail, and the scenery just can not be beat.

While in town, be sure to explore more of Richwood's backcountry by mule; we really enjoyed our mule-pulled wagon tour deep into the Monongahela Forest, where we spotted several black bears.

Length: 16.5 miles

Surface: Packed stone, varied roughness

Allowed Uses: H, Mt. B, E

County: Nicholas

Endpoints: Richwood and Allingdale

Access Points: Richwood F/W, Fenwick F/W, Holcomb F/W, Allingdale

Note: Follows Cherry and Gauley Rivers

Contact: Four Season Outfitters 304-846-2862

Trail Roughness: ★★

Scenery: ★★★

Directions:

From Charleston, WV to Richwood: Take I-79 North to Exit 57. Turn onto US 19 South and take to WV 55 East. Turn left on WV 55 East and take into Richwood. At the red light in Richwood, turn right and go downhill toward the depot. The depot is on the right about 1 1/2 blocks away. Parking is available on local streets or in a shopping center about two blocks south of depot. From the depot, the trail goes west toward Holcomb and the mouth of the Cranberry River.

To Holcomb: The rail trail crosses WV 55 just east of the Girder Bridge crossing of Cherry River, about 6 miles west of Richwood, or

20 miles east of US 19. Small yellow trailhead signs are posted on WV 55, and parking is available on either side of the road. From WV 55 facing Cherry River bridge, right is northwest toward the Mouth of the Cranberry River, and left is east toward Richwood.

To Fenwick: Trailhead is located at the intersection of WV 39 and WV 55, west of WV 39 Cherry River bridge and between WV 55 and the Cherry River. Trailhead parking is next to the Fenwick Post Office. From the bridge turn left and immediately left again to trailhead. Trail goes underneath bridge between WV 55 and the river. From WV 55 facing Cherry River and the post office, right is west toward Holcomb and the Mouth of the Cranberry River, and left is east toward Richwood.

WHERE TO STAY AND DINE:

Four Seasons Lodge
Marlington Road
Richwood, WV 26261
304-846-4605

Snowshoe Mountain Resort
10 Snowshoe Drive
Snowshoe, WV 26209
304-572-1000

Elk River Touring Center
US 219
Slatyfork, WV 26291
304-572-3771

OTHER:

Cranberry Glades Botanical Area
Rt. 39
Richwood, WV 21626
304-653-4826

25. ELK RIVER RAIL TRAIL

The shortest of West Virginia's rail trails, Elk River still warrants mentioning because of its urban setting in the state's capital city.

The one-mile packed gravel trail that runs along the Elk River is one of the best spots for cycling with young children, or for jogging and short hikes. Both of my kids did some of their first off-road rides on this trail, even though the trail does have a steep but very short rise on it.

The trail is located on the outskirts of Coonskin Park, a favorite destination for children because of its multiple playgrounds, a lake with pedal boats and ducks, a game room and a skateboard park. The trail is convenient for parents wanting to share a short, non-stressful bike ride with kids. The packed gravel makes for easy riding for bikes pulling trailers or even for hardy pre-schoolers on bikes with training wheels. The short distance makes it ideal for adults wanting to get back into shape by starting with an easy, non-intimidating ride. For a special treat, ride through the main road through Coonskin Park during the holiday season, and you'll be greeted by hundreds of Christmas light displays, some of which are visible from the trail.

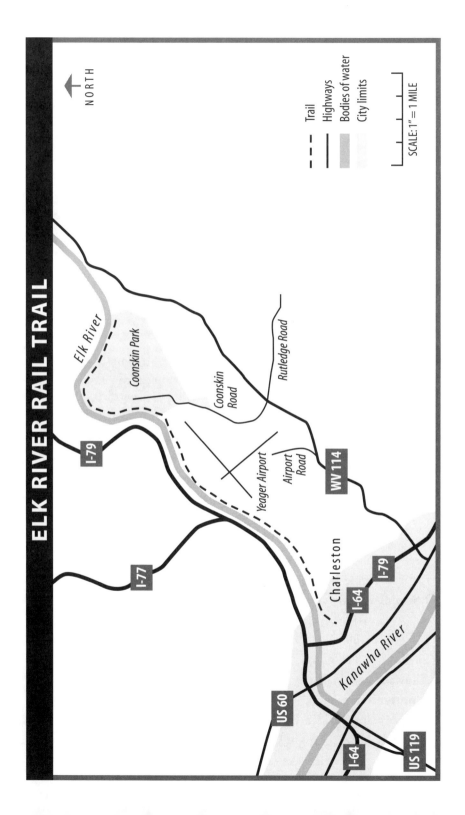

Future plans include extending the Elk River Trail in Coonskin Park to connect to other areas of Charleston. A group called "The Friends of the Kanawha Trestle Trail" is currently working on developing a trail that will be a multi–use, non-motorized trail connecting the Mound in South Charleston to the State Capitol complex. Plans are also afoot to connect the Elk River Valley via Coonskin Park through to Capitol Market and Kanawha City via the 35th Street Bridge. This rail trail system will preserve and restore two historic and unique rail structures that are eligible to be listed on the National Historic Register. One is the CSX Trestle over the Kanawha River, built in 1907 with a combined steel truss and timber construction that is over 4,200 feet long. The other is the Whipple Bridge over the Elk River, built in 1890. The Whipple Bridge is an early example of iron construction in bridges.

Length: 1 mile
Surface: Packed gravel
Allowed uses: H, B
County: Kanawha
Endpoints: Coonskin Park
Access Points: Coonskin Park F/W

Contact: Coonskin Park 304-341-8000,
         www.kanawhacountyparks.com
Trail Roughness: ★
Scenery: ★

Directions:

To Coonskin Park: Take I-64/I-77 to Charleston. Take the WV 114/Greenbrier Street Exit 99 at the State Capitol. Turn left onto WV 114 N/Greenbrier Street if coming from I-77 North, and if approaching from I-77 South, turn right onto WV 114. Take WV 114, bearing right before the airport turnoff, and go to the traffic light. Turn left onto Coonskin Drive. Follow signs to Coonskin Park. Follow main road through park. Go past the pond and turn left into parking area. Park here. You will see the concession area at the far end of the parking lot. The trail is located directly behind the concession area.

WHERE TO STAY AND DINE:

The Marriott
200 Lee Street E.
Charleston, WV 25301
304-345-6500

Ramada Charleston
400 2nd Avenue SW
Charleston, WV 25303
304-744-4641

Blossom Deli & Soda Fountain
904 Quarrier Street
Charleston, WV 25301
304-345-2233

Lola's Pizza
1038 Bridge Road
Charleston, WV 25314
304-343-5652

Bridge Road Bistro
915 Bridge Road
Charleston, WV 25314
304-720-3500

Joe Fazio's
1008 Bullitt Street
Charleston, WV 25301-1004
304- 344-3071

Charleston Town Center Mall Food Court
Court Street
Charleston, WV 25301
304-345-9526

26. HAWKS NEST RAIL TRAIL

This 1.8-mile rail trail actually makes for an awesome downhill ride/hike—and you can escape the very significant 550-foot climb back up the mountain by hopping on the Pipestem Tram or by arranging a shuttle. This trail, which can easily be a calm, scenic descent or a raging, adrenaline-packed downhill (depending on what type of rider you are), starts in downtown Ansted along Hawks Nest Road.

When Hawks Nest State Park is open and for a small fee, the aerial tram can be taken back to the main park on US 60 (they will allow the bicycle in the tram gondola). You can then bike east about 1.5 on US 60 back to Ansted. There is automobile access at the bottom of the trail if the tram is closed.

We found this trail to be extremely well maintained by the city of Ansted, and it was obvious to us the town takes great pride in it. The trail ends at the New River, where you'll see the Hawks Nest Railroad Crossing, a picnic area and the Hawks Nest Nature Center. The Nature

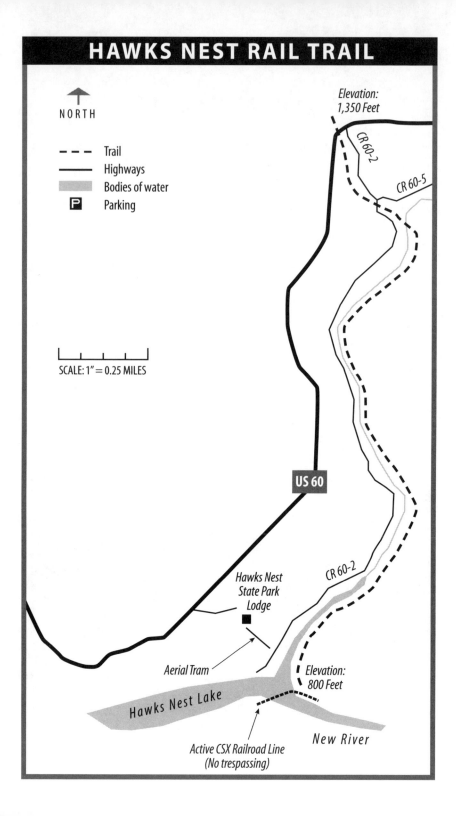

HAWKS NEST RAIL TRAIL

NORTH

- - - Trail
——— Highways
░░░ Bodies of water
P Parking

SCALE: 1" = 0.25 MILES

Elevation:
1,350 Feet

CR 60-2

CR 60-5

US 60

CR 60-2

Hawks Nest
State Park
Lodge

Aerial Tram

Elevation:
800 Feet

Hawks Nest Lake

New River

Active CSX Railroad Line
(No trespassing)

Center features live reptile and amphibian exhibits as well as an on-site naturalist to provide information and answer questions. Along the way you'll see some waterfalls spilling over the mountainside, several old coke ovens, an antiquated water tower, as well as some magnificent vistas of the New River Gorge area.

If you have your own shuttle, your driver will drive down River Road, which runs alongside the trail, winding down the mountain to the same spot. Tram operation is seasonal and requires a ticket purchase,

so check with the park lodge for more information. Restrooms are available at both ends.

Work has begun to extend the Hawks Nest Trail through the New River Gorge. The trail will go from the Hawks Nest State Park, attaching to the existing Hawks Nest Rail Trail and continue into the New River National Park, adding at least six miles to the existing trail. This is a collaborative project between the National Park Service, Hawks Nest State Park and the town of Ansted.

While in Ansted, be sure to check out the world-famous Mystery Hole, as well as the Ansted Museum and the Contentment Museum. Ansted was the hilltop home of many settlers in the 1790s, many of whom were quite wealthy due to the rich coal seams nearby. On a knoll in the center of town, the mansion of William Nelson Page still stands as evidence of the area's once-thriving coal business.

Length: 1.8 miles
Surface: Pea gravel
Allowed uses: H, B
County: Fayette
Endpoints: Ansted and Hawks Nest Lake
Access Points: Ansted F/W

Note: Follows Mills Creek
Contact: Town of Ansted 304-658-5901, anstedmayor@verizon.net
Trail Roughness: ★★
Scenery: ★★★

Directions:

From Charleston: Take I-64/I-77 toward Beckley (Portions toll). Take US 60/WV 61 (Exit 85) toward Chelyan/Cedar Grove. Follow US 60 into Ansted. Turn left at Cemetery Road as you drive into Ansted; it will take you by the Rite-Aid. (To identify the turn, look for the Veteran Memorial on your right.) You will turn left again in about 200 feet. This takes you beneath US 60 to the trailhead.

WHERE TO STAY AND DINE:

Hawks Nest State Park Lodge
177 W Main Street
Ansted, WV 25812
304-658-5212

Midland Trail Motel
Rt. 60
Ansted, WV 25812
304-658-5065

River's View Restaurant at Hawks Nest State Park
177 West Main Street
Ansted, WV 25812
304-658-5212

Gino's Pizza
425 Main Street
Ansted, WV 25812
Phone 304-658-5234

Blue Smoke Salsa
119 East Main Street
Ansted, WV 25812
(888) 725-7298

Smokey's On the Gorge
1 Ames Heights Road
Lansing, WV 25862
304-574-4905

Tudor's Biscuit World
425 Main Street
Ansted, WV 25812
304-658-5235

OTHER:

Ansted Museum
110 E. Main Street
Ansted, WV 25812
Phone 304-658-5901

Contentment Museum
Rt. 60 Main Street
Ansted, WV 25812
Phone 304-658-5695

The Mystery Hole
Rt. 60
Ansted, WV 25812
304-658-9101

27. NARROW GAUGE RAIL TRAIL

Even the superintendent at Babcock State Park will tell you most people don't think of this as a rail trail. Narrow Gauge bears little resemblance to the flat, wide, easy-to-ride rail trails that traverse the state. This trail wasn't a permanent railway track, but rather a temporary trail used solely to bring timber out of the woods. Thus, it is more of a winding single-track trail with lots of roots and rocks. The trail requires the rider to have some technical experience and a true off-road mountain bike with wide knobby tires. However, the trail is worth including in your plans because of its heritage as part of the backcountry railways system and for its location in the beautiful Babcock State Park, home of the beautiful widely-photographed gristmill.

You should park in the lot near the gristmill and ride/hike back up toward the park entrance, accessing the trail on the eastern end. (The trail can be ridden in either direction, but this way gets some of the climbing out of the way on the park road, and has more downhill on the trail.)

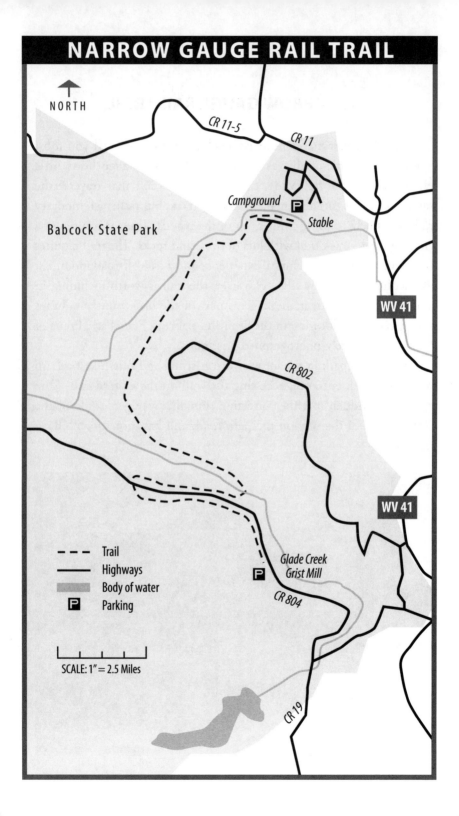

NARROW GAUGE RAIL TRAIL

NORTH

CR 11-5

CR 11

Campground

Stable

Babcock State Park

WV 41

CR 802

WV 41

- - - Trail
— Highways
Body of water
P Parking

Glade Creek
Grist Mill

CR 804

SCALE: 1" = 2.5 Miles

CR 19

The first part of your ride/ hike will be along Glade Creek, which will be on your left. When you come to the cabin area, you will head down a paved downhill section before reaching the Narrow Gauge trailhead. The first part of the trail descends fairly easily off the hillside. But, be on alert, the next section becomes very technical and quite dangerous if you do not have strong off-road skills. At times you will be riding/hiking on a very narrow ridge with Glade Creek on your right. Exercise extreme caution; the drop-off is very steep. Eventually you will come to a piece of the trail where you will see remnants of abandoned railway. There is a hike-a-bike up a hill shortly after this, followed by a fun downhill with a great surprise at the bottom—a very cool suspension bridge crossing the creek. If you are riding, you will need to walk your bike across the bridge. Stop on the bridge for a view of the picturesque creek—with a garden of giant boulders and choppy whitewater. You'll also have to lug your bike up the steep embankment on the other side. You'll soon make a sharp switchback to the left, which will take you up a service road back to the park entrance.

Length: 2.5 miles
Surface: Soil over old ballast and cinders
Allowed uses: H, Mt. B
County: Fayette
Endpoints: Babcock State Park
Access Points: Babcock State Park W
Contact: Babcock State Park 304-438-3004, babcock@mail.wvnet.edu,
    www.babcocksp.com

Trail Roughness: ★★★★
Scenery: ★★★

Directions:

To reach both ends of the trail, from US 19, take the US 60 exit and head east for 10 miles to WV 41, heading south.

The trail can be accessed from the campground, which is 2 miles south of US 60 at Clifftop (the trail begins on the service road between the campgrounds and the stables). This entrance is open only in the summer.

The trail also can be accessed from the main park entrance, a little farther south on WV 41, behind Cabin #13. Follow the signs to Cabin #13 from the entrance: go behind the Glade Creek Grist Mill and follow that road (Old Sewell Road) past the cabins to the official start of the trail at the fork of the creek. The trail is downhill from the cabins to the campground.

WHERE TO STAY AND DINE:

Babcock State Park
Rt. 60
Clifftop, WV 25831
304-438-3004

White Water Inn
RR 3 Box 431
Fayetteville, WV 25840
304-574-2998

Mill Creek Cabins
Milroy Grose Road
Lansing, WV 25862
304-658-5005

River's View Restaurant at Hawks Nest State Park
177 West Main Street
Ansted, WV 25812
304-658-4444

Gumbo's Cajun Restaurant
103 S. Court Street
Fayetteville, WV 25840
304-574-4704

OTHER:

Ace Adventure Center
Minden Road
Oak Hill, WV 25901
888-ACE-RAFT
304-469-2651

Tamarack: The Best of West Virginia
One Tamarack Park
Beckley, WV 25801
304-256-6843
1-88 TAMARACK

Ansted Museum
110 E. Main Street
Ansted, WV 25812
304-658-5901

Contentment Museum
Rt. 60 Main Street
Ansted, WV 25812
304-658-5695

The Mystery Hole
Rt. 60
Ansted, WV 25812
304-658-9101

28. BROOKLYN TO SOUTHSIDE JUNCTION

The Brooklyn to Southside Junction Trail should be ridden beginning at the Brooklyn trailhead heading south along the New River as an out-and-back. The trail winds through the abandoned mining towns of Red Ash and Rush Run. The trail was once an important transportation corridor used to haul coal from the remote New River Gorge. As you ride or hike you will never be more than 100 yards from the New River. The area is heavily forested with plenty of large oak trees, rhododendron and evergreens. This trail is a favorite of mountain bikers who like the rough riding caused by exposed railroad ties along the way.

What we found most impressive about this trail is the evidence of "melding." Melding refers to keeping the integrity of the rail bed by working the remaining wood and steel into the trail. At times you are riding/hiking directly over the exposed railroad ties, making for a bumpy

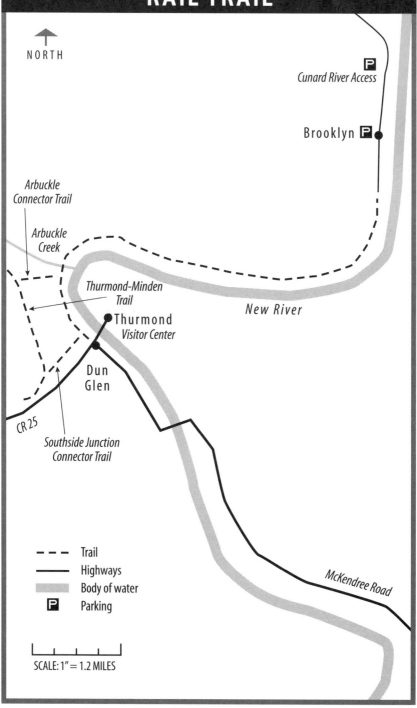

BROOKLYN-SOUTHSIDE JUNCTION RAIL TRAIL

NORTH

P
Cunard River Access

Brooklyn P

Arbuckle
Connector Trail

Arbuckle
Creek

Thurmond-Minden
Trail

New River

Thurmond
Visitor Center

Dun
Glen

CR 25

Southside Junction
Connector Trail

McKendree Road

- - - Trail
——— Highways
Body of water
P Parking

SCALE: 1" = 1.2 MILES

and somewhat tricky ride. While making your way over and around the wood beams, you are suddenly very aware that you are riding/hiking along a path used by locomotives in the 19th century. All the while you are high above the raging waters of the New River and its tributaries, passing old coke ovens and abandoned buildings, crossing charming wooden bridges and going through tunnels of rhododendron.

The 5.8-mile trail ends at a set of active railroad tracks at the Southside Junction. The trail technically extends past these tracks, but currently there is no safe or legal crossing, so riders/hikers should keep clear of the tracks. For this reason, this trail should be ridden/hiked as an out and back and only starting at Brooklyn.

The Thurmond Visitors Center just across the river at the southern end of the trail is a must-see while in the area. The restored passenger train station, located at CR 25/2 in Thurmond in the heart of the New River Gorge, serves as a museum and visitor center operated by the National Park Service (NPS). During the first two decades of the 1900s,

Thurmond was a classic coal boomtown with the huge amounts of coal brought in from area mines. Fifteen passenger trains a day came through town—its depot serving as many as 95,000 passengers a year. The town's stores and saloons did a remarkable business, and its hotels and boarding houses were constantly overflowing. Today, Thurmond remains surprisingly untouched by modern development.

For those wanting to ride both the Rend trail and the Brooklyn to Southside Junction trail, they are super close to each other. The Arbuckle Connector trail is only .3 miles long and connects the two trails. But, it is currently prohibited to ride your bike on this trail. You should walk your bike on this trail anyway, as it is rough and has steps to climb. If you do decide to ride both trails, use this route as the railroad tracks at the south end of both trails are on private property and should be respected.

Length: 5.8 miles
Surface: Soil and packed ballast
Allowed Uses: H, B
County: Fayette
Endpoints: Brooklyn and Southside Junction
Access Points: Brooklyn F/W
Note: Follows New River
Contact: New River Gorge National River 304-438-3004,
            www.nps.gov/neri
Trail Roughness: ★★★
Scenery: ★★★★

Directions:
    From Beckley, WV to Brooklyn trailhead: Take US 19 North to Fayetteville. Take WV 16 South through Fayetteville and turn left onto Gatewood Road. Turn left at the Cunard turnoff and follow signs to Cunard River Access. Once you reach the river access area, continue 1 mile up the gravel road to the Brooklyn trailhead, where parking is available.

    The Southside Junction end is not recommended as the start as it is an active rail line perpendicular to the trail. Using this as a trailhead often blocks access to the line, making crossing hazardous. Use Brooklyn as the start of an out-and-back trip.

WHERE TO STAY AND DINE:

Ace Adventure Center
Minden Road
Oak Hill, WV 25901
1-888-Ace Raft
304-469-2651

White Water Inn
RR 3
Fayetteville, WV 25840
304-574-2998

Hawks Nest State Park Lodge
177 W. Main Street
Ansted, WV 25812
304-658-5212

Chico's Restaurant
2027 Main Street E.
Oak Hill, WV 25901
304-469-6505

29. REND TRAIL
(FORMERLY THURMOND TO MINDEN)

The 3.4-mile recently renamed Rend (Thurmond to Minden) rail trail offers scenic vistas of the New River Gorge and more evidence of historic railways. The Rend Trail is one of the most popular trails in the New River Gorge, and for good reason. The trail is wide, well-maintained, and includes numerous bridges and awesome vistas. The trail follows the Arbuckle Branch Railroad corridor (built in 1906) along the banks of three bodies of water from the old mining community of Minden to the historic railroad town of Thurmond. The trail begins along the very beautiful Arbuckle Creek and follows the water to its confluence with the New River.

After following the New River for a short distance, the trail heads south toward Thurmond, along the peaceful banks of Dunloup Creek. The trail ends at a parking lot near a popular fishing hole. While the Thurmond-Minden Trail is excellent for bicycling and hiking, beware: a set of stairs built around the remains of a rockslide will hinder your

REND TRAIL (FORMERLY THURMOND-MINDEN TRAIL)

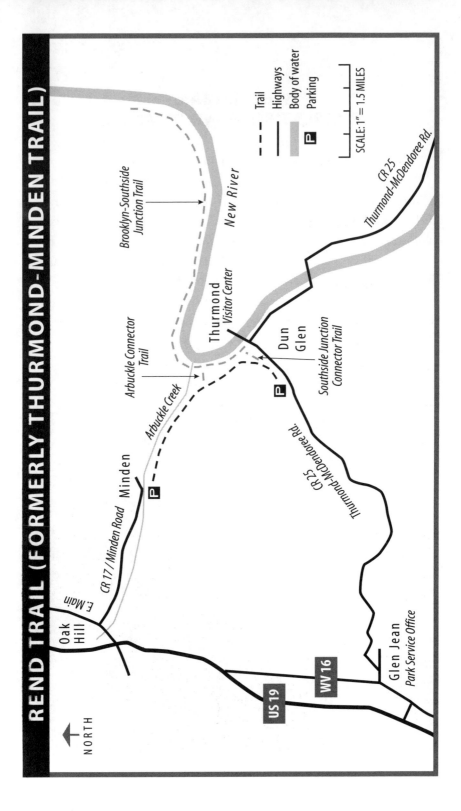

NORTH

Brooklyn-Southside Junction Trail

New River

Thurmond
Visitor Center

Arbuckle Connector Trail

Arbuckle Creek

Minden

Dun Glen

Southside Junction Connector Trail

CR 17 / Minden Road

E. Main

Oak Hill

Thurmond-McDendoree Rd. (CR 25)

CR 25
Thurmond-McDendoree Rd.

US 19

WV 16

Glen Jean
Park Service Office

--- Trail
— Highways
▬ Body of water
P Parking

SCALE: 1" = 1.5 MILES

journey if you are unable to carry your bike up and down the steep steps. Also, wood and steel melding, along with some rocks and roots, make the trail fun to ride/hike but also a little challenging.

I rode part of this trail when competing in the Captain Thurmond's Triathlon and found myself being distracted from competition by the awesome scenery around me. The mostly flat trail passes through several large rock outcroppings. I had been told that one of the rocks features a "locally famous" likeness of President McKinley (though no one could tell me exactly where it was on the trail). Local legend has it that the nature-made sculpture was discovered the day before McKinley was shot. I wasn't able to find it, but consider it a challenge to put West Virginia's own Mount Rushmore on the map.

The Thurmond Visitors Center just across the river at the southern end of the trail is a must-see while in the area. The restored passenger train station, located at CR 25/2 in Thurmond in the heart of the New River Gorge, serves as a museum and visitor center operated by the National Park Service (NPS). During the first two decades of the 1900s, Thurmond was a classic boomtown with the huge amounts of coal brought in from area mines. Fifteen passenger trains a day came through town—its depot serving as many as 95,000 passengers a year.

The town's stores and saloons did a remarkable business, and its hotels and boarding houses were constantly overflowing. Today, Thurmond remains surprisingly untouched by modern development.

For those wanting to ride both the Rend trail and the Brooklyn to Southside Junction trail, they are super close to each other. The Arbuckle Connector trail is only .3 miles long and connects the the two trails. Biking the .3 mile Arbuckle Connector is prohibited, which is wise as it is rough and has steps. Walking your bike is the only option. If you do decide to ride both trails, use this route as the railroad tracks at the south end of both trails is private property and should be respected.

Length: 3.4 miles
Surface: Packed dirt, small gravel/varied roughness
Allowed uses: H, B
County: Fayette
Endpoints: Thurmond and Minden
Access Points: Minden F/W, Thurmond F/W
Note: Trestles, views of New River
Contact: New River Gorge National River 304-438-3004,
    katy_miller@nps.gov, www.nps.gov/neri
Trail Roughness: ★★★
Scenery: ★★★★

Directions:
    From Beckley, WV to the Thurmond trailhead: Take US 19 North. Take the Thurmond-Glen Jean exit and turn left onto WV 25. Go half a mile to Glen Jean, following the signs for the Thurmond-Minden Trail, located 5 miles outside of Glen Jean off WV 25.
    From Beckley, WV to the Minden trailhead: Go north on US 19. Take the Oak Hill/Main Street exit and turn right onto East Main Street at the end of the ramp. Turn left at Minden Road and follow it for 2 miles. Take a right across a small bridge to the Minden trailhead.

WHERE TO STAY AND DINE:

Ace Adventure Center
Minden Road
Oak Hill, WV 25901
1-888-Ace Raft
304-469-2651

White Water Inn
RR 3
Fayetteville, WV 25840
304-574-2998

Hawks Nest State Park Lodge
177 W Main Street
Ansted, WV 25812
304-658-5212

OTHER:

Ace Adventure Center/Whitewater Rafting
Minden Road
Oak Hill, WV 25901
1-888-Ace Raft
304-469-2651

Tamarack: The Best of West Virginia
One Tamarack Park
Beckley, WV 25801
304-256-6843
1-88 TAMARACK

30. BECKLEY RAIL TRAIL
(LEWIS N. McMANUS MEMORIAL HONOR TRAIL)

The Beckley Rail Trail, also known as the Lewis McManus Memorial Honor Trail, is the perfect city trail, frequented by runners, walkers, dog walkers, as well as cyclists. Beckley, the largest city in Raleigh County, is often called the "Gateway to Southern West Virginia." While in Beckley, a must-see is Tamarack, West Virginia's arts and crafts showcase. Plan to spend a few hours exploring Tamarack; the complex also hosts an excellent food court, serving dishes from the Greenbrier chef.

Once on the trail, you will find parts of the pristine highland town is straight out of a storybook. Though you'll pass through buildings and ride alongside traffic, the green rolling hills serve as a majestic backdrop.

BECKLEY RAIL TRAIL

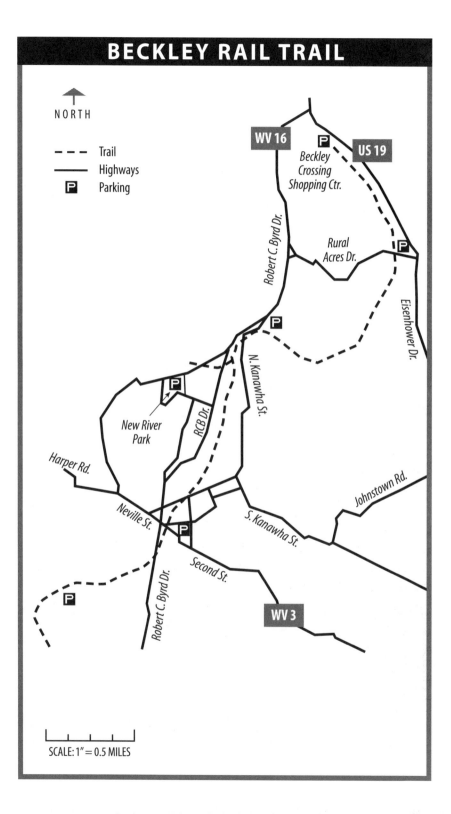

One big plus for this trail is that it is lighted, making it available for night riding/hiking, but always use the buddy system.

The trail begins across from the Beckley Crossing Shopping Center and makes its way through town, eventually ending in Mabscott. Though most of the trail is very well-marked, there is one spot that is a little unclear. At the first fork you come to, make sure you stay left. Also be cautious, as there are several traffic crossings. We found the trail to be well-patrolled, but be careful, as it does cross through several sketchy parts of town. The trail is an easy out-and-back. At the end, you have the choice to ride down a short road to downtown Mabscott, population 1,400, before turning around and heading back.

The trail follows the old Piney River and Paint Creek Railroad branch line, which was taken over by the Chesapeake and Ohio Railway in 1918. This wide, paved trail crosses from Mabscott to Cranberry Creek Crossing with a spur over Robert C. Byrd Drive that extends to the New River Park. Coming from the Beckley Crossing Mall trailhead, the spur will be on your right, shortly after 2 miles into the ride. From the turn, it is a short distance to the park.

Length: 3.6 miles
Surface: Asphalt
Allowed uses: H, B, S, A
County: Raleigh
Road Access: WV 16 & WV 3, and WV 16 & US 19
Endpoints: Beckley Crossing Shopping Center and Mabscott
Access Points: Many streets in Beckley F/W
Note: Trail is lighted for night use
Contact: Southern West Virginia CVB 304-252-2244 or
    1-800-VISITWV, www.beckley.org or www.visitwv.com
Trail Roughness: ★
Scenery: ★

Directions:
    To Beckley: Take I-64 /I-77 toward Beckley (Portions toll.) Take Exit 48/Mall exit. End at Beckley. From Exit 48 you take WV 16 to US

19—there is a small parking lot (dirt) across from Beckley Crossings Shopping Center (this is a strip mall not the large mall you will see when you come off of Exit 48) at trailhead.

WHERE TO STAY AND DINE:

Microtel Inn & Suites
1001 S. Eisenhower Drive
Beckley, WV 25801
304-255-2200

Days Inn
127 Ontario Drive
Mt Hope, WV 25880
304-877-6455

Econo Lodge
1909 Harper Road
Beckley, WV 25801
304-255-2161 or 888-259-8542

Country Inn & Suites
2120 Harper Road
Beckley, WV 25801
304-252-5100 or 800-456-4000

Pagoda Motel
1114 Harper Road
Beckley, WV 25801
304-253-7373

Pinecrest Motel
230 N. Eisenhower Drive
Beckley, WV 25801
304-255-1577

Morgan's Food & Spirits
1924 Harper Road
Beckley, WV 25801
304-255-1511

OTHER:

Ace Adventure Center
Minden Road
Oak Hill, WV 25901
888-ACE-RAFT
304-469-2651

Tamarack: The Best of West Virginia
One Tamarack Park
Beckley, WV 25801
304-256-6843
1-88 TAMARACK

31. WHITE OAK RAIL TRAIL

This is a short trail, but has plenty of variety. The scenery changes from being in the middle of town to a very rural setting pretty quickly, and to a pleasant subdivision.

The western two-mile section is paved, wide and smooth. There are several road crossings on this trail, and traffic could be an issue at times. We used caution and had no problems on any of the three trips we made on this trail though. The last 1.5 miles is rough with loose gravel, however, we were assured at press time that the city was scheduled to pave this section within months.

We found it easiest to start in town and the middle of the trail and bike out and back to both ends, but for describing the trail, I'll start at the Woodbridge Road end of the trail.

Starting at the northern end of the trail off of Woodbridge Road, the wide paved trail immediately begins a gentle climb for 1.4 miles. While noticeable, it was quite gradual and easy to maintain a good speed. At about 9/10 of a mile, you'll see the middle school on the right. A bench is beside the trail with a nice view of the grounds here. When going back, downhill, you can coast and maintain your speed for the entire 9/10th a mile.

Just pass the school is the busiest road crossing on the trail. Use caution and walk here. Just past the main road on the right is a great place to stop for a treat. Tom's Diary has been in business since 1961 and has been run by three generations of Tom's.

At 1.3 miles you will see the bright yellow-orange depot on the left. There are a couple benches on the loading platform and each time we rode past, walkers and bikers occupied them all. The depot is in the process of being restored. An old worn out engine and a caboose sit forlornly off to the right. The caboose looked like it had been converted at one point to an ice cream stand, but now displays a for sale sign on it. Be careful, the trail crosses Central Avenue just past the depot.

Another two tenths of a mile and you are at the crossing for

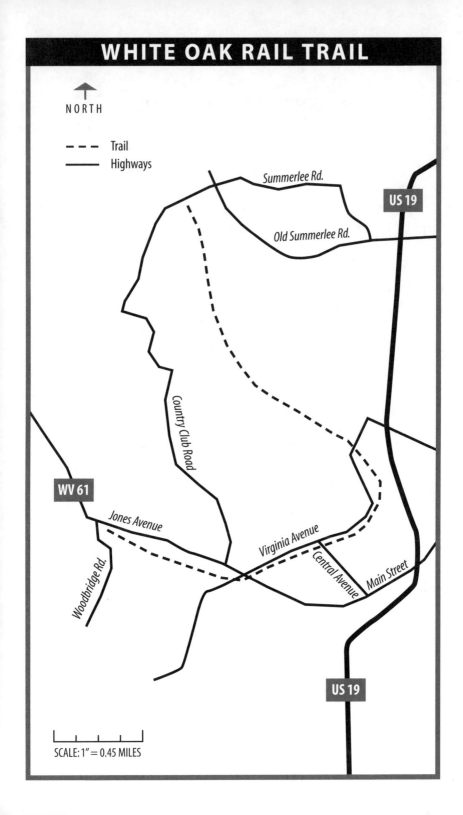

WHITE OAK RAIL TRAIL

NORTH

- - - Trail
—— Highways

Summerlee Rd.

US 19

Old Summerlee Rd.

Country Club Road

WV 61

Jones Avenue

Virginia Avenue

Central Avenue

Main Street

Woodbridge Rd.

US 19

SCALE: 1" = 0.45 MILES

Summerlee Ave., at 1.5 miles. At 1.6 miles you cross Sherry's Junction and start to leave the town behind. At 2.0 miles the pavement ends and a Pizza Hut and Holiday Inn are located off the road to the right.

Across this road is where the section that should be paved by now starts. Several spots had mud puddles and the gravel was large in many places, and it made for a bumpy ride. The trail ends at Summerlee Road. While the trail looks like it continues on when we stopped to cross the road, it only goes a few yards before abruptly ending in a driveway. While rough, this section was fun to ride as we saw a golf course from the trail, and plenty of wildlife and butterflies. It was a nice contrast to riding in town just a few minutes before.

Length: 3.4 miles
Surface: 2 miles paved with additional 1.4 miles unpaved
Allowed Uses: H, B, S, A
County: Fayette
Access Points: Woodbridge Road, Jones Avenue/Route 61 F/W,
   Central Avenue, Summerlee Avenue, Virginia Street F/W.
Contact: City of Oak Hill 304-469-9541
Trail Roughness: paved ★★★★ / unpaved ★
Scenery: ★★★★

Directions: From Charleston: Take I-64 East/I-77 South to Exit 60 for Mossy/Oak Hill. Turn left onto WV 612 East/CR 15/4. Stay on WV 612 East. Then turn left on CR 1/5/Scarbro Road. This takes you into town to Main Street. Turn left on Main Street, then left again in two blocks on Jones Avenue and go about 5 blocks and turn left into Collins Park. Parking is also available a few blocks further down Jones Avenue at Collins Middle School.

WHERE TO STAY AND DINE:

Ace Adventure Center
Minden Road
Oak Hill, WV 25901
1-888-Ace Raft

Tom's
554 Jones Avenue
Oak Hill, WV 25901
304-469-6260

Chico's Restaurant
2027 Main Street East
Oak Hill, WV 25901
304-469-6505

32. RAIL TRAIL EPIC RIDES

1) Pennsylvania to Parkersburg: North to South, then East to West (Mon River Trail North, Caperton Trail, Mon River South, Marion County Trail, West Fork River Trail, North Bend Rail Trail)

—Mon River Trail North (Morgantown) at PA line—Problem is accessing the trail across the PA border. Look for connection off US 119. Trail may be complete soon to Point Marion, PA, which would offer easier access. Most people ride north to PA line from Morgantown on this trail, or just start from Morgantown.

—Alternate start (but wouldn't be PA): Start in Reedsville on the eastern end of Deckers Creek Trail (see Chapter 9). This is east of Morgantown on WV 7 and is roughly 19 miles, mostly downhill to Morgantown with about 1.800 feet of elevation drop.

—At Caperton Trail in Morgantown (connects at Ruby McQuain Riverfront Park), go South (left) on Caperton Trail/Mon River South. About 20 miles to Prickett's Fort Park, north of Fairmont.

—Connect there onto Marion County Trail (2.5 miles) to downtown Fairmont. Road ride a few miles at most to Mary Lou Retton Youth Park.

—Connect there onto north end of West Fork River Trail. Go south about 17 miles to Shinnston.

—Get a shuttle or road ride US 119 to Clarksburg, then east on US 50 a few miles to Wolf Summit, the eastern end of North Bend Rail Trail.

—Enter North Bend Rail Trail west. Goes all the way to Parkersburg, approximately 72 miles.

2) Heart of Appalachian Mountains North to South Epic ride: Thomas to Lewisburg.

(Blackwater Canyon Rail Trail, Allegheny Highlands Trail, West Fork Rail Trail, Greenbrier River Trail)

—Begin in Thomas on Blackwater Canyon Rail Trail. Go southwest about 10 miles. At Hendricks, the trail becomes Allegheny Highlands Rail Trail. Go approximately 23 miles to Elkins.

—Now the tricky part. You need to somehow (shuttle or road ride) get to Glady on the northern end of the West Fork Rail Trail. If biking, you'll have 3 or so miles on busy US 219 before turning left at Midland on CR 25. Then at CR 22 go right and then huff it over Cheat Mountain to Glady. If you drive (as we did), you might consider skipping Glady and driving straight to the other end of the West Fork Rail Trail in Durbin as the trip is on easier roads.

—From Durbin, shuttle or road ride to Cass, at WV 28 South and WV 66 West. Enter north end of Greenbrier Rail Trail. Ride south, approximately 77 miles to Caldwell (near Lewisburg).

APPENDIX

BIKE SHOPS

BECKLEY

Ride-N-Slide Sports
403 Second Street
Beckley, WV 25801
304-253-5202

X-Treme Sports
2978 Robert C. Byrd Dive
Beckley, WV 25801
304-255-2664
Email: info@extremewv.com
Website: www.xtremewv.com

BUCKHANNON

Fat Tire Cycle
33 East Main Street
Buckhannon, WV 26201
304-472-5882
Email: fattire@fattirecycle.com
Website:www.fattirecycle.com

CAIRO

Country Trails
Cairo, WV 26337
304-628-3100

CALDWELL

Free Spirit Adventures and Bike Shop
HC 30, Box 183-C
Caldwell, WV 24925
Phone: 304-536-0333

Fax: 304-536-1580
Email: freespirit@inetone.net
Website: www.freespiritadventures.com

CASS

Cass Bikes
Cass, WV 24927
304-456-4429

High Country Connections
HC 61, Box 156
Cass, WV 24927
304-456-4429

CHARLESTON

Charleston Bicycle Center
409 53rd Street
Charleston, WV 25304
304-925-8348

CLARKSBURG

Holy Moses Bike Shop
645 West Park Street
Clarksburg, WV 26301
304-622-7235

DAVIS

Blackwater Bikes
Main Street
Davis, WV 26260
304-259-5286
Email: info@blackwaterbikes.com

FAYETTEVILLE

**New River Bike and Touring
  Company**
102 Keller Avenue
Fayetteville, WV 25840
304-574-2453
Website: www.newriverbike.com

HUNTINGTON

Huntington Bicycle Center
623 16th Street
Huntington, WV 25701
304-525-5312
Email: info@huntingtonbicyclecenter.
  com

Jeff's Bike Shop
740 6th Avenue
Huntington, WV 25701
304-522-2453
Website: www.jeffsbikeshop.com

Sniders
238 4th Avenue
Huntington, WV 25701
304-522-0471

MORGANTOWN

Pathfinder of WV
235 High Street
Morgantown, WV 26505
304-296-0076
Email: pathfinderwv@aol.com

Wamsley Cycles
709 Beechurst Avenue
Morgantown, WV 26505
304-296-2447
Website: www.WamsleyCycles.com

Whitetail Cycle & Fitness
54 Clay Street
Wharf District, on the Caperton
  Riverton Trail
Morgantown, WV 26505
304-296-0076

PARKERSBURG

Bob's Bicycle Shop
2207 Camden Avenue
Parkersburg, WV 26104
304-424-6317

RAVENSWOOD

MAK Repairs
110 Royal Street
Ravenswood, WV 26164
304-273-4222

SEEBERT

Jack Horner's Corner Bike Rental
HC 64, Box 521
Seebert, WV 26946
304-653-4515

SHEPERDSTOWN

Billy Brothers Mountain Bikes
P.O. Box 3159
Shepherdstown, WV 25443
304-876-1254

SLATYFORK

Elk River Touring Center
HC 69 Box 7
Slatyfork, WV 26291
304-572-3771
Email: ertc@ertc.com
Website: www.ertc.com

SNOWSHOE

Snowshoe Mountain Biking Center at Silver Creek
P.O. Box 10
Snowshoe, WV 26209
304-572-6766
Email: info@snowshoemtn.com
Website: www.snowshoemtn.com

Snowshoe Mountain Biking Center at the Inn
P.O. Box 10
Snowshoe, WV 26209
04-572-6538
Email: info@snowshoemtn.com
Website: www.snowshoemtn.com

SOUTH CHARLESTON

Dive Tech & Sports
614 D. Street
South Charleston, WV 25303
304-744-2453

ST. ALBANS

John's Cyclery
309 MacCorkle Avenue
St. Albans, WV 25177
304-727-2180

THURMOND

Thurmond Supply
Thurmond, WV 25936
304-469-2380

VIENNA

Skier's Edge Sports Loft
499 Grand Central Avenue
Vienna, WV 26105
304-428-4754
Email: skiersedge@eurekanet.com

Vienna Bicycle Shop
2910 Grand Central Avenue
Vienna, WV 26105
304-295-5469
Email: ben@viennabicycleshop.com

WHEELING

Wheelcraft, Ltd.
2817 National Road
Wheeling, WV 26003
304-242-2100

BIKE ASSOCIATIONS

Mountain State Wheelers
Contact: Bill and Mary Shultz
304-342-2517
Email: MBider1055@msn.com
Website: www.mountainstatewheelers.
    org

West Virginia Mountain Bike Association
Phone: 304-288-0512
Executive Director: Greg Moore
Email: Exec@WVMBA.com
Website: www.wvmba.com

West Virginia Rail Trails Council
Email: bikenhike@gillumhouse.com
Website: www.wvrtc.org

CYCLING WEBSITES:

Adventure Cycling Association: www.adv-cycling.org
West Virginia Mountain Bike Association (WVMBA):
   www.wvmba.com
Beech Fork Association of Trails (BFAT): www.bikeBFAT.com
International Mountain Bicycling Association (IMBA):
   www.imba.com
Country Roads Cyclists, formerly Harrison County Bicycle
   Association (HCBA) based in north-central West Virginia:
   www.crcyclists.org
National Rails to Trails Conservancy: www.railtrails.org
Monongahela River Trails Conservancy (MRTC): montrails.org
North Bend Rails to Trails Foundation: www.northbendrailtrail.com
Fun Places to Cycle in West Virginia: www.wvbike.org
West Virginia Trails Coalition (WVTC): www.wvtrails.org

RAIL TRAIL WEBSITES:

Allegheny Highlands Trail: www.highlandstrail.org
Beckley Rail Trail: www.beckley.org / www.visitwv.com
Elk River Rail Trail: www.kanawhacountyparks.com
Narrow Gauge Rail Trail: www.babcocksp.com
Hawks Nest Rail Trail: www.hawksnestsp.com
Harrison County Southern Rail Trail: www.wvrtc.org
Harrison County Hike and Bike Rail Trail: www.healthywv.com
West Fork River Rail Trail: www.mcparc.com
Williams River Trail: www.traillink.com
Gauley Mountain Trail: www.traillink.com
Brooklyn to Southside Junction: www.newriverwv.com
Rend Trail (Thurmond-Minden Trail): www.newriverwv.com
Marion County Trail: www.mcparc.com
Mon River North & South: www.americantrails.org / www.montrails.
   org
Caperton Trail: www.americantrails.org / www.montrails.org

Deckers Creek Trail: www.americantrails.org / www.montrails.org
Cheat Lake Rail Trail: www.montrails.org
East Wetzel Rail Trail: www.healthywv.com
North Marion Rail Trail: www.manningtonmainstreet.org
Panhandle Rail Trail: www.wvrtc.org / www.panhandletrail.org
Wellsburg Yankee Rail Trail: www.healthywv.com
Brooke Pioneer Rail Trail: www.brookepioneertrail.org
Wheeling Heritage Rail Trails: www.cityofwheelingwv.org
Glen Dale to Moundsville Trail: www.healthywv.com
Barnum Rail Trail: www.mineralcountywv.com
Blackwater Canyon Trail: www.wvbike.org
West Fork Rail Trail: www.destinationdurbin.com
Cranberry Tri-Rivers Rail Trail: www.wvrtc.org
Greenbrier River Rail Trail: www.greenbrierrivertrail.com
North Bend Rail Trail: www.northbendrailtrail.com

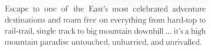

Adventure

Abundant recreation at North Bend State Park

North Bend State Park

Year-round lodge and rental cabins
Restaurant with home-style cooking
Campgrounds • Lake • Fishing
Events and special packages
Nearby North Bend Rail Trail

Wild and Wonderful
West Virginia
State Parks & Forests
www.northbendsp.com
304.643.2931

Ride one of West Virginia's most successful rail-to-trail conversions - the popul[ar] Greenbrier River Trail. Hear the nearby free-flowing Greenbrier River as you thread yo[ur] way through 78 miles of lush pastures and thick forests alive with brightly colored bird[s,] curious wildlife, and extraordinary wildflowers.

For maps and lodging information
www.GreenbrierRiverTrail.com
800.336.7009

Bike your way into beauti-ful, rugged mountains an[d] find miles of endless dirt roads and railroad grade[s.] Trails in Pocahontas County have epic climbs and white-knuckling dow[n] hills to challenge the mo[st] experienced riders.

Welcome to real mountain biking!

For special mountain biking brochure and maps
call us at 800.336.7009
or visit us on the Web at
PocahontasCountyWV.com

POCAHONTAS
COUNTY
West Virginia ®

Nature's Mountain Playgrou[nd]

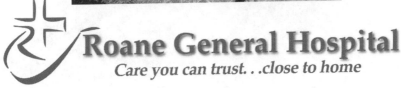

409 53rd Street, S.E.
Charleston, West Virginia 25304
(304)925-8348

ABOUT THE AUTHOR

Robin Broughton's background in adventure communications includes being a competitive athlete and a professional journalist. With a Ph.D. in Interpersonal Communication and currently a professor of communications and media studies at West Virginia State University, Robin formerly worked as a reporter. Robin is the author of *Mountain State Biker's Guide to West Virginia* (Quarrier Press 2006) and has written for *Mountain Bike Action, Velo News, Dirt Rag, Wild Wonderful West Virginia* and *Bike Midwest.* Robin has directed and promoted two mountain bike races and she has taught mountain biking clinics throughout the state. She has raced mountain bikes for the past 15 years, and was on a national championship mountain biking and adventure triathlon team. Robin has mountain biked in Australia, Europe, Central America and Africa, as well as throughout the eastern and western United States. Her most recent adventure includes climbing Mt. Kilimanjaro in East Africa accompanied by several WVSU students.